Family Food in 2002-03

A National Statistics Publication by Defra

LONDON : TSO

Published with the permission of the Department for Environment, Food and Rural Affairs on behalf of the Controller of Her Majesty's Stationery Office.

© Crown Copyright 2004

All rights reserved.

Copyright in the typographical arrangement and design is vested in the Crown. Applications for reproduction should be made in writing to the Copyright Unit, Her Majesty's Stationery Office, St Clements House, 2-16 Colegate, Norwich NR3 1BQ.

First published 2004

ISBN 0 11 243084 8

A National Statistics Publication
National Statistics are produced to high professional standards set out in the National Statistics Code of Practice. They undergo regular quality assurance reviews to ensure that they meet customer needs. They are produced free from any political interference.

For general enquiries about National Statistics, contact the National Statistics Customer Contact Centre on
0845 601 3034
minicom: 01633 812399
E-mail: info@statistics.gov.uk
Fax: 01633 652747
Post: Room D115
Government Buildings
Cardiff Road
Newport
NP10 8XG

Published by TSO (The Stationery Office) and available from:

Online
www.tso.co.uk/bookshop

Mail, Telephone, Fax & E-mail
TSO
PO Box 29, Norwich NR3 1GN
Telephone orders/General enquiries: 0870 600 5522
Fax orders: 0870 600 5533
E-mail: book.orders@tso.co.uk
Textphone 0870 240 3701

TSO Shops
123 Kingsway, London WC2B 6PQ
020 7242 6393 Fax 020 7242 6394
68-69 Bull Street, Birmingham B4 6AD
0121 236 9696 Fax 0121 236 9699
9-21 Princess Street, Manchester M60 8AS
0161 834 7201 Fax 0161 833 0634
16 Arthur Street, Belfast BT1 4GD
028 9023 8451 Fax 028 9023 5401
18-19 High Street, Cardiff CF10 1PT
029 2039 5548 Fax 029 2038 4347
71 Lothian Road, Edinburgh EH3 9AZ
0870 606 5566 Fax 0870 606 5588

TSO Accredited Agents
(see Yellow Pages)

and through good booksellers

Contents

Preface — v

Chapter 1: **Key results in Family Food in 2002-03** — 1
    Headlines — 1
    Household consumption of fruit and vegetables — 1
    Trends in intakes of energy, fat and added sugars — 3
    Energy and nutrient Intakes in 2002-03 — 5
    Household consumption in 2002-03 — 8
    Eating Out consumption in 2002-03 — 9
    Expenditure on all food and drink in 2002-03 — 9

Chapter 2: **Long term trends in Household Food** — 11
    Household consumption since 1975 — 11
    Consumption of fruit and vegetables since 1975 — 16
    Intakes from household food and drink since 1975 — 18
    Percentage contributions to energy intake from household food — 22

Chapter 3: **Trends in expenditure on food and drink** — 25
    Expenditure from 1975 to 2002-03 — 25
    Expenditure in real terms — 25
    Prices — 27

Chapter 4: **Food eaten out** — 29
    Eating out consumption in 2002-03 — 29
    Intakes from eating out since 1994 — 30
    Eating out intakes in 2002-03 — 32

Chapter 5: **Household consumption in 2002-03** — 33
    Headline changes — 33
    Milk, cream and cheese — 33
    Meat, fish and eggs — 34
    Sugar and preserves — 35
    Fruit and vegetables — 35
    Bread, cereals and cereal products — 36
    Beverages and miscellaneous foods — 37
    Soft and alcoholic drinks and confectionery — 37
    Takeaway foods — 38

Chapter 6: **Regional Comparisons** — 41
    United Kingdom countries — 41
    England regions — 45

Chapter 7: **Demographic comparisons** — 51
    Income quintile — 51
    Household composition — 55
    Age group of household reference person — 58
    Age at which household reference person ceased full-time education — 63
    Ethnic origin of household reference person — 65
    Occupation of household reference person — 69
    Economic activity of household reference person — 73

Chapter 8:	**Related official statistics**	77
	Comparison of dietary surveys	77
	Family Spending	81
	Food prices	81
	Consumer Trends	82
Chapter 9:	**Adjustments to the National Food Survey estimates**	83
	Background	83
	Defra original scaling (published in October 2003)	84
	Defra revised scaling	84
	Applying the adjustments back to 1974	84
	Impact of the adjustments	85

Preface

This report presents estimates of average consumption, expenditure and energy and nutrient intakes from food and drink in the United Kingdom in 2002-03, along with historical trends. The period covered in the latest year 2002-03 is from 1 April 2002 until 31 March 2003. In 2001-02 the National Food Survey was replaced by the Expenditure and Food Survey. At the same time coverage was extended to include food and drink eaten out. Limited estimates of food eaten out are available from the National Food Survey back to 1994. The latest data are sourced from the Expenditure and Food Survey. First results for the United Kingdom were published in a Statistics Notice on 24th June 2004.

This report covers household food and food eaten out analysed by region and demographic characteristics (household composition, income quintiles, age of household reference person, age at which household reference person ceased full time education, occupation, ethnic origin and economic status of household reference person).

Estimates for eating out in 2001-02 and 2002-03 are included in the report and integrated with estimates for household food and drink (household food covers all food and drink brought into the household, including takeaways brought home).

Free food such as school meals and work-provided meals and snacks are not included in the estimates for 2001-02 and 2002-03. Occurrences of these are recorded in the survey and estimates of consumption will be made for future reports.

Confectionery, alcoholic drinks and soft drinks brought home are included in household food from 1992 onwards. In 1996 the survey was extended to cover Northern Ireland – prior to 1996 the quoted averages relate to Great Britain only but generally this makes little difference.

Historical estimates of household food consumption between 1974 and 2000 have been adjusted to the level of estimates from the Family Expenditure Survey in 2000, which are broadly comparable with estimates from the Expenditure and Food Survey. This has partially corrected for under-reporting in the National Food Survey. Under-reporting is considered to be lower in the Expenditure and Food Survey due on the one hand to its focus on recording expenditure and on the other hand that everyone over seven years old completes a diary. Whilst estimates of household consumption from the National Food Survey have been adjusted a break in the series in 2001-02 remains. This must be borne in mind when interpreting reported changes between the year 2000 (source National Food Survey) and the year 2001-02 (source Expenditure and Food Survey).

All tables, many with fuller details, can be found free of charge on the family food page of the statistics section of the Defra website at:
http://statistics.defra.gov.uk/esg/publications/efs/default.asp

Chapter 1: Key results in Family Food in 2002-03

Headlines

- Average energy intake per person in the UK is unchanged in 2002-03 compared with the previous year, although it has been declining since 1964, see chart 1.2.

- The percentage of energy derived from fat, excluding energy from alcohol, is slightly lower than in the previous year at 37.6 per cent in 2002-03, but this level is still above the recommended level of 35 per cent, see table 1.3.

- The percentage of energy derived from saturated fatty acids, excluding energy from alcohol, is slightly lower at 14.7 per cent in 2002-03 but this level is still above the recommended level of 11 per cent.

- The percentage of energy derived from non-milk extrinsic sugars (added sugars), including energy from alcohol, is slightly higher at 15.1 per cent in 2002-03.

- Potato consumption is down 4.4 per cent in 2002-03, see table 1.5.

- Fruit consumption is up 4.3 per cent in 2002-03.

- Fruit and vegetable consumption in 2002-03 is estimated to be 2.5 per cent higher at 2305 grams per person per week. This equates to an average of 4.1 portions per person per day but is based on the weight of the produce as purchased and includes all fruit juice and baked beans for which only the first 80 grams are included in the 5 A DAY programme, see chart 1.1. The Health Survey for England which lines up with the 5 A DAY definition estimates that on average adults consumed 3.4 portions per day in 2002, see chapter 8.

- Milk consumption continues to fall, down 1.6 per cent in 2002-03, see chart 2.1.

- Consumption of alcoholic drinks outside the home is 4.0 per cent lower in 2002-03, see chapter 4. Household consumption is also lower.

Household consumption of fruit and vegetables

Fruit and vegetables are considered important for a healthy diet. Chart 2.1 shows that the trend in average household consumption per person of fruit and vegetables has generally been increasing since at least 1974. The horizontal line at 2800 grams represents 5 portions of 80 grams per day. It is not equivalent to the 5 A Day measure because it is based on the weight of produce as purchased and includes all fruit juice and all baked beans, for which only the first 80 grams are included in the 5 A DAY programme, and it excludes fruit and vegetables eaten out.

Household consumption of fruit and vegetables rose by 2.5 per cent in 2002-03 to an average of 2336 grams per person per week. This equates to an average of 4.1 portions per person per day but these portions include all fruit juice and baked beans.

The drop in 2001-02 is probably due to higher prices that year for fruit and vegetables in the shops. However, it may also be affected by the change of data source in April 2001 from the National Food Survey to the Expenditure and Food Survey.

Consumption of fruit rose by 4.3 per cent in 2002-03 to an average of 1206 grams per person per week.

The increasing trend since 1974 is being driven mainly by increased consumption of fresh fruit and fruit juices. Consumption of fresh green vegetables and processed vegetables has been falling. Consumption of non-green fresh vegetables, which includes onions, carrots, cucumbers and mushrooms has been rising.

Chart 1.1 Consumption of fruit and vegetables

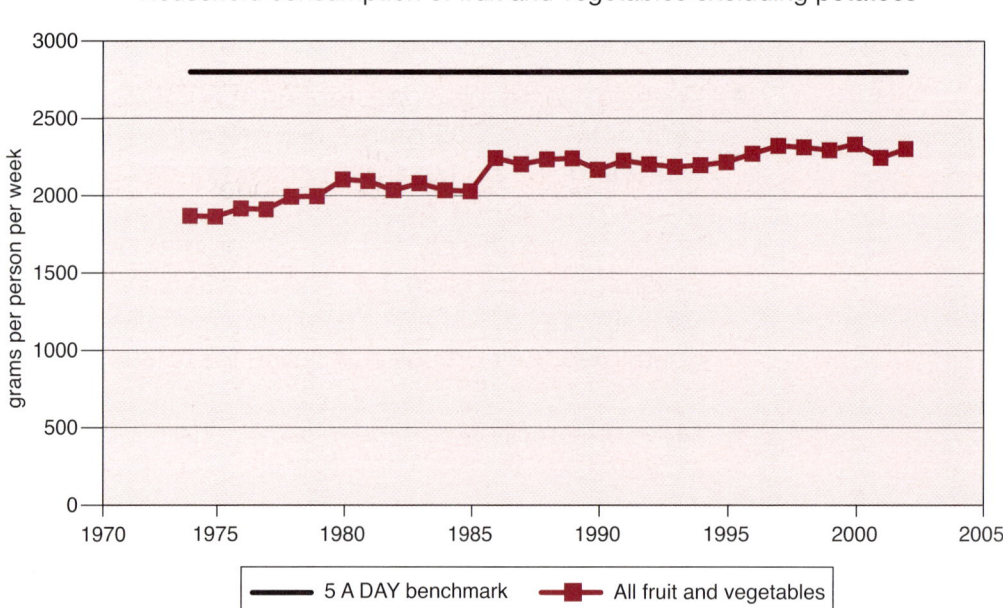

Table 1.1 Consumption of fruit and vegetables

UK average consumption of fruit and vegetables	Adjusted National Food Survey				Expenditure & Food Survey	
	1975	1985	1995	2000	2001-02	2002-03
					grams per person per week	
Fruit and vegetables exc. potatoes	1868	2032	2219	2336	2248	2305
Fruit	738	825	1068	1189	1156	1206
Fresh fruit	511	540	693	765	750	794
Processed fruit	228	286	375	424	406	413
Fresh green vegetables	341	287	233	246	229	231
Other fresh vegetables	405	461	486	506	502	505
Processed vegetables exc. potatoes	385	459	431	395	360	363
Potatoes	1378	1340	1077	1002	907	867

Potatoes are not included in the 5 A DAY programme or chart 1.1 because they are a starchy food. However, household consumption of potatoes has been falling. More details on trends in consumption of fruit and vegetables including potatoes are shown in a special section in Chapter 2.

Trends in intakes of energy, fat and added sugars

Average energy intake from all food and drink remained the same in 2002-03 at an average of 2301 Kcals per person per day.

The long term trend in energy intake from food and drink is downwards as shown in Chart 1.2. The series has gradually broadened in scope, from household food excluding confectionery, soft drinks and alcoholic drinks in 1940, to all food and drink from 2001-02 onwards. However, the downward trend since 1964 is clear in all components of the chart except the latest two years.

Chart 1.2 Average energy intake since 1940

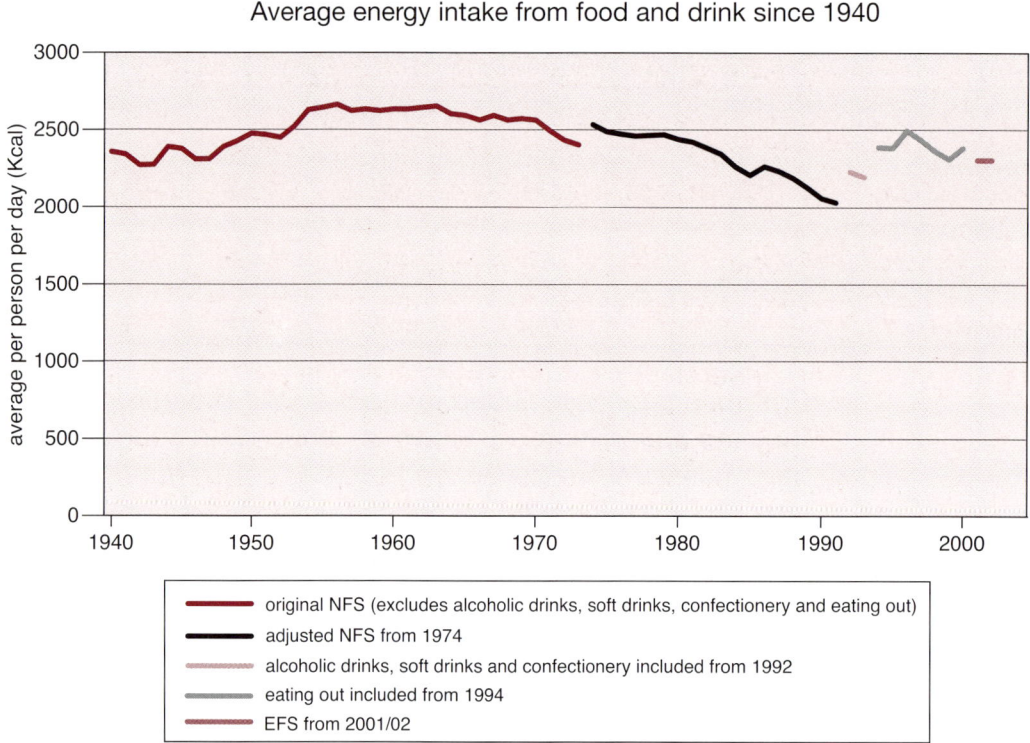

NFS: National Food Survey 1940 to 2000
EFS: Expenditure and Food Survey from 2001/02

Given the general decline in energy intake it is helpful to look at the percentage of energy obtained from different sources.

Table 1.2 shows that the percentage of energy obtained from fat, including energy from alcohol, has been in decline from 38.7 per cent in 1994 to 36.3 per cent in 2002-03. The population average recommended level is 33 per cent. A similar decline is seen in the percentage of energy derived from saturated fatty acids, from 15.2 per cent in 1994 to 14.2 per cent in 2002-03, compared with the population average recommendation of 10 per cent. The percentage of energy obtained from non-milk extrinsic sugars (added sugars) has not been in decline although it fluctuates from year to year. Its level in 2002-03 at 15.1 per cent is above the population average recommended level of 10 per cent.

Table 1.2 Percentage of energy intake from fat and added sugars from all food and drink[a]

		1994	1995	1996	1997	1998	1999	2000	2001-02	2002-03
								average per person per day		
energy intake, including energy from alcohol	Kcal	2387	2383	2496	2433	2362	2311	2382	2301	2301
from fat	%	38.7	37.8	37.7	37.4	37.3	36.5	36.4	36.6	36.3
from saturated fatty acids	%	15.2	15.1	14.9	14.8	14.8	14.5	14.6	14.3	14.2
from non-milk extrinsic sugars	%	15.1	15.1	15.4	15.3	15.0	14.9	15.4	14.9	15.1

(a) Eating out estimates from 1994 to 2000 are based on the National Food Survey and considered less reliable

Energy and nutrient intakes in 2002-03

Table 1.3 shows energy and nutrient intakes in 2002-03 from household food and food eaten out, including confectionery, soft drinks and alcoholic drinks. Whilst changes in intakes are generally small from year to year there are notable decreases in intakes of saturated and poly-unsaturated fatty acids, sodium, β carotene and vitamin E. There are notable increases in non-milk extrinsic sugars (added sugars), fibre, thiamin and vitamin C.

Average intake of fibre, expressed as non-starch polysaccharides, was 14.4 grams per person per day, an increase of 0.9 per cent.

In general about 9 per cent of energy and nutrient intakes come from food and drink eaten out with the notable exception of alcohol where it is 37 per cent. The general level was also 9 per cent in 2001-02. Estimates from the National Food Survey are less reliable but indicate that broadly 10 per cent of energy intake has come from eating out since data was first collected in 1994 – see chapter 4.

The estimates show that the percentages of intakes from food and drink eaten out are lower for calcium, riboflavin, iron, fibre, vitamin B12, retinol equivalent and vitamin D, with eating out contributing between 6 and 7 per cent of total food and drink intakes. The percentages of intakes from food and drink eaten out are higher for added sugars, vitamin B6, niacin equivalent and folate as well as for alcohol.

Table 1.3 also shows the percentages of energy derived from fat, fatty acids and carbohydrate in two ways – excluding energy from alcohol and including energy from alcohol.

The percentage of energy obtained from fat, including energy from alcohol, has fallen by 0.3 percentage points to 36.3 per cent whilst that from carbohydrates has risen 0.3 percentage points to 46.8 per cent. This compares with the population average recommendations of 33 per cent of total energy intake from fat, 10 per cent from saturated fatty acids and 47 per cent from carbohydrate.

The percentage of energy obtained from fat, excluding energy from alcohol, has fallen by 0.3 percentage points to 37.6 per cent whilst that from carbohydrates has risen 0.3 percentage points to 48.5 per cent. This compares with the population average recommendations of 35 per cent of total energy intake from fat and 11 per cent from saturated fatty acids.

Food eaten out provides a higher proportion of energy from fat than does household food. Excluding the contribution of alcohol, 39.3 per cent of energy from food eaten out is derived from fat compared to 37.4 per cent of energy from household food.

Table 1.3 Energy and nutrient intakes in 2002-03

UK average energy and nutrient intakes from food and drink in 2002-03[a]		household food	food eaten out	all food and drink	% change since 2001-02	% from food eaten out
					intake per person per day	
Energy	kcal	2091	210	2301	+0.0	9.1
	MJ	8.8	0.9	9.7	+0.0	9.1
Vegetable protein	g	28.2				
Animal protein	g	43.1				
Total Protein	g	71.3	6.2	77.6	+0.1	8.0
Fat	g	85.0	7.9	92.9	−0.7	8.5
Fatty acids:						
Saturates	g	33.6	2.8	36.4	−0.8	7.7
Mono-unsaturates	g	30.6	3.1	33.7	−0.6	9.1
Poly-unsaturates	g	15.0	1.5	16.5	−1.2	9.3
Cholesterol	mg	235	24	259	−0.6	9.4
Carbohydrate[b]	g	265	23	287	+0.7	7.9
Total sugars	g	124	12	136	+0.8	8.9
Non-milk extrinsic sugars	g	82	10	92	+1.0	11.3
Starch	g	141	11	152	+0.5	7.1
Fibre[c]	g	13.4	0.9	14.4	+0.9	6.6
Alcohol	g	6.9	4.1	11.0	−1.6	37.2
Calcium	mg	932	62	993	−0.2	6.2
Iron	mg	11.1	0.8	11.9	+1.0	6.8
Zinc	mg	8.5	0.7	9.2	+0.4	7.7
Magnesium	mg	258	24	282	+0.1	8.6
Sodium[d]	g	2.80	0.23	3.03	−1.9	7.6
Potassium	g	2.87	0.26	3.14	−0.4	8.4
Thiamin	mg	1.51	0.12	1.63	+0.9	7.3
Riboflavin	mg	1.84	0.12	1.97	−0.2	6.3
Niacin Equivalent	mg	30.4	3.5	33.9	+0.1	10.3
Vitamin B6	mg	2.2	0.3	2.4	−0.8	10.6
Vitamin B12	µg	5.8	0.4	6.2	−0.8	6.5
Folate	µg	259	29	288	+0.5	10.2
Vitamin C	mg	68	5	74	+0.7	7.0
Vitamin A:						
Retinol	µg	500	33	533	−1.3	6.2
β-carotene	µg	1753	141	1894	−2.8	7.4
Retinol equivalent	µg	800	57	856	−1.0	6.6
Vitamin D	µg	3.26	0.24	3.51	−0.3	6.9
Vitamin E	mg	11.13	1.19	12.32	−1.6	9.6
		contributions to all energy from food & drink excluding alcohol				
Fat	%	37.4	39.3	37.6	−0.8	
Fatty acids:						
Saturates	%	14.8	13.8	14.7	−0.9	
Mono-unsaturates	%	13.5	15.2	13.6	−0.7	
Poly-unsaturates	%	6.6	7.6	6.7	−1.3	
Carbohydrate	%	48.6	47.1	48.5	+0.6	
		contributions to all energy from food & drink				
Fat	%	36.6	33.9	36.3	−0.7	
Fatty acids:						
Saturates	%	14.4	11.9	14.2	−0.8	
Mono-unsaturates	%	13.2	13.1	13.2	−0.6	
Poly-unsaturates	%	6.4	6.5	6.4	−1.2	
Carbohydrate	%	47.5	40.7	46.8	+0.6	

(a) Contributions from pharmaceutical sources are not recorded by the Survey
(b) Available carbohydrate, calculated as monosaccharide
(c) As non-starch polysaccharides
(d) Excludes sodium from table salt

Table 1.4 shows how different household food groups contribute to intakes from household food. The major sources of energy are non-carcase meat and meat products, bread and cereals. Fat intake is obtained mainly from purchases of fats and oils such as butter and other spreads but also from meat and meat products and milk and milk products. Calcium comes mainly from milk and bread and iron mainly from bread and cereals. Added sugars come mainly from purchases of sugar and preserves, from soft drinks and from confectionery. Sodium (excluding that from table salt) comes mainly from other meat and meat products, bread and food in the "other food" category (mainly sauces and ice cream). Vitamin C is mainly from both processed and fresh fruit whilst β carotene comes mainly from vegetables. More detailed estimates are available on the Defra website.

Table 1.4 Nutrient intakes from selected household foods

Average intake per person per day from household food and drink in 2002-03

	Energy	Fat	Saturated fatty acids	Calcium	Iron	Non-milk extrinsic sugars	Sodium	Vitamin C	β carotene	Vitamin A (Retinol equiv.)
	Kcal	grams	grams	mg	mg	grams	grams	mg	μg	μg
Milk and cream	178	8.0	5.0	350	0.2	2.7	0.136	4.0	43	93
Cheese	58	4.8	3.0	97	0.0	0.0	0.115	0.0	21	53
Carcase meat	63	4.3	1.8	2	0.4	0.0	0.020	0.0	0	1
Other meat and meat products	221	14.1	5.1	32	1.2	0.1	0.603	2.4	73	166
Fish	29	1.4	0.3	14	0.2	0.0	0.075	0.0	5	4
Eggs	18	1.3	0.4	7	0.2	0.0	0.017	0.0	0	23
Fats	188	20.6	6.1	4	0.0	0.2	0.108	0.0	85	163
Sugar and preserves	75	0.0	0.0	3	0.1	19.9	0.004	0.4	1	0
Fresh potatoes	50	0.1	0.0	4	0.3	0.0	0.006	4.5	0	0
Fresh green vegetables	6	0.1	0.0	10	0.2	0.0	0.002	2.9	79	13
Other fresh vegetables	15	0.2	0.0	13	0.3	0.0	0.008	5.0	935	156
Processed vegetables	128	5.4	1.8	25	0.9	1.0	0.251	6.4	272	49
Fresh fruit	47	0.4	0.1	12	0.2	0.0	0.003	16.0	33	6
Processed fruit	45	1.5	0.3	9	0.3	6.1	0.012	17.3	11	2
Bread	248	2.6	0.6	164	1.9	0.1	0.537	0.0	1	4
Flour	30	0.1	0.0	12	0.2	0.0	0.000	0.0	0	0
Cakes, buns and pastries	81	3.2	1.4	17	0.3	5.9	0.070	0.1	3	10
Biscuits	120	5.6	2.8	25	0.5	6.2	0.090	0.0	0	0
Other cereal products	221	4.2	1.5	68	2.6	4.9	0.283	2.2	29	19
Beverages	6	0.1	0.0	7	0.2	0.7	0.007	0.0	0	2
Other food	71	3.8	1.4	21	0.4	5.8	0.412	0.6	80	17
Soft drinks	59	0.0	0.0	9	0.0	15.8	0.018	6.6	74	12
Confectionery	78	3.1	1.7	18	0.2	11.1	0.018	0.0	6	5
Alcoholic drinks	54	0.0	0.0	7	0.3	1.3	0.007	0.0	0	0
Total household intake	2091	85	34	932	11	82	2.801	68	1753	800

Household consumption in 2002-03

Table 1.5 Household consumption

UK average consumption of household food and drink		2001-02	2002-03	RSE Indicator[b] for 2002-03	%change
Number of households in sample		7473	6927		
Number of persons in sample		18122	16586		
		grams per person per week unless otherwise stated			
Milk and cream	(ml)	2023	1990	✓✓✓	−1.6
Cheese		112	112	✓✓✓	−0.4
Carcase meat		229	230	✓✓✓	+0.4
Other meat and meat products		803	809	✓✓✓	+0.8
Fish		157	154	✓✓✓	−1.4
Eggs	(no.)	1.65	1.66	✓✓✓	+0.7
Fats		196	190	✓✓✓	−3.2
Sugar and preserves		147	146	✓✓✓	−0.6
Potatoes		907	867	✓✓✓	−4.4
Vegetables exc. potatoes		1092	1099	✓✓✓	+0.7
Fruit		1156	1206	✓✓✓	+4.3
Cereals		1655	1665	✓✓✓	+0.6
Beverages		60	58	✓✓✓	−2.7
Soft drinks[a]	(ml)	1744	1756	✓✓✓	+0.7
Alcoholic drinks[c]	(ml)	735	726	✓✓	−1.2
Confectionery		128	127	✓✓✓	−0.8

(a) Converted to unconcentrated equivalent by applying a factor of 5 to concentrated and low calorie concentrated soft drinks
(b) Relative standard error. 3 ticks <2.5%, 2 ticks 2.5%-5%, 1 tick 5%-10%, no ticks 10%-20%
(c) Assuming consumption is only by over thirteens average consumption of alcoholic drinks in 2002-03 would be 879ml per person over thirteen per week

The ticks indicate the reliability of the 2002-03 estimates. At this level of aggregation the sampling errors are small; three ticks indicates that the relative standard error of the estimate is less than 2.5 per cent. Alcoholic drinks is the least reliable estimate with a relative standard error of 2.6 per cent.

The changes in consumption since the previous year are generally small and rarely statistically significant. Whilst not statistically significant they are our best estimate of the changes going on. Chapter 2 puts these changes into the longer term perspective where on-going trends can be seen.

Consumption of potatoes is estimated to have fallen by 4.4 per cent whilst that of fruit is estimated to have risen by 4.3 per cent. There is an estimated fall in consumption of fats and oils of 3.2 per cent as purchased for household consumption. Consumption of milk and cream is estimated to have fallen by 1.6 per cent.

Eating Out consumption in 2002-03

Table 1.6 Eating out consumption

UK average consumption of food and drink eaten out		2001-02	2002-03	%change
		grams per person per week unless otherwise stated		
Number of households in sample		7473	6927	−7.3
Number of persons in sample		18122	16586	−8.5
Ethnic meals[a]		22	22	+1.9
Meat and meat products		94	95	+0.9
Fish and fish products		15	14	−4.5
Cheese and egg dishes and pizza		25	26	+3.9
Potatoes		88	85	−3.3
Vegetables		34	34	+1.9
Sandwiches		80	80	+0.6
Ice cream, desserts and cakes		31	32	+2.1
Beverages	(ml)	154	147	−5.0
Soft drinks inc. milk drinks	(ml)	373	376	+0.8
Alcoholic drinks	(ml)	732	702	−4.0
Confectionery		23	22	−2.3

(a) Indian, Chinese, Thai and other "ethnic" meals

Eating out estimates are only available in detail since 2001-02 and are presented in full in chapter 4. The main component is alcoholic drinks which is estimated to have fallen by 4.0 per cent in 2002-03.

Expenditure on all food and drink in 2002-03

Table 1.7 Expenditure on food and drink

UK average expenditure on food and drink	2001-02	2002-03	% change
Number of households in sample	7473	6927	−7.3
Number of persons in sample	18122	16586	−8.5
household food			*£ per person per week*
Milk and cream	1.44	1.47	+2.3
Cheese	0.57	0.58	+2.0
Carcase meat	1.03	1.06	+2.8
Other meat and meat products	3.55	3.64	+2.6
Fish	0.93	0.93	+0.1
Eggs	0.17	0.17	+3.5
Fats	0.36	0.37	+1.1
Sugar and preserves	0.15	0.16	+4.1
Potatoes	1.04	0.99	−5.1
Vegetables exc. potatoes	1.67	1.70	+1.9
Fruit	1.50	1.59	+6.5
Cereals	3.57	3.66	+2.5
Beverages	0.44	0.42	−3.7
Soft drinks	0.72	0.74	+2.7
Alcoholic drinks	2.44	2.49	+1.9
Confectionery	0.81	0.77	−5.1
Other food	1.13	1.16	+2.7
Food and Drink exc. alcoholic drinks	19.08	19.42	+1.8
All household food and drink	21.52	21.91	+1.8
food eaten out			
Food and drink less alcohol	6.98	7.21	+3.4
Alcoholic drinks	3.71	3.73	+0.5
All food and drink eaten out	10.68	10.94	+2.4
all food			
Food and drink less alcohol	26.06	26.63	+2.2
Alcoholic drinks	6.15	6.21	+1.0
All Food and drink	32.21	32.85	+2.0

Overall average expenditure on food and drink including eating out has risen by 2.0 per cent in 2002-03 to £32.85 per person per week. The rise is more or less in line with general inflation; the retail price index estimates a rise of 2.1 per cent over this period.

Average expenditure on eating out excluding alcoholic drinks has risen by 3.4 per cent to £7.21 per person per week, whilst that on alcoholic drinks has risen by less than inflation to £3.73 per person per week. It is important to note that these averages include everyone in the United Kingdom.

Average expenditure on household food and drink has increased by 1.8 per cent to £21.91 per person per week. In real terms this represents a small drop. Of the household items, the largest rise is in fruit where average expenditure is up by 6.5 per cent to £1.59 per person per week. Expenditure on confectionery has fallen by 5.1 per cent to an average of 77 pence per person per week. Details of trends in expenditure since 1975 are shown in chapter 3.

Chapter 2: Long term trends in household food

The figures in this section are based on adjusted National Food Survey results up to 2000 and Expenditure and Food Survey results from 2001-02 onwards. For more detail on how the adjustments to the National Food Survey results were carried out see chapter 9 of this report.

Food and drink eaten out is excluded from this section since historical data are not available.

More detailed series for all years from 1974 to 2002-03 can be found on the Defra website along with estimates for some types of food and some nutritional intakes going back to 1940.

Household consumption since 1975

Table 2.1 shows the trend in UK consumption of selected food groups from 1975 onwards. Household consumption as measured by the National Food Survey and the Expenditure and Food Survey includes food and drink purchased and brought into the home. It is measured in the form it is purchased in, for example, eggs purchased and later used to make a cake will be recorded under eggs and not under cakes. However, if a ready-made cake is purchased, it is recorded under cakes. For consumption, no adjustment is made for non-edible parts of food items such as skins, peels and bones nor for other food waste.

The main changes in household consumption between 1975 and 2002-03 are:

- Milk consumption has fallen by 33 per cent.

- Egg consumption has fallen by over 50 per cent.

- Potato consumption has fallen by over 50 per cent.

- Bread consumption has fallen by over 25 per cent.

- Fresh fruit consumption has risen by over 50 per cent

- Processed fruit consumption has risen by over 80 per cent.

- Consumption of cereal products (excluding bread, buns and cakes) has risen by over 90 per cent.

Table 2.1 Consumption of household food since 1975

UK Average household consumption		Adjusted National Food Survey				Expenditure & Food Survey	
		1975	1985	1995	2000	2001-02	2002-03
						per person per week	
Wholemilk	ml	2715	1904	818	680	599	555
Other milk and cream	ml	272	510	1427	1484	1424	1435
Cheese	g	107	111	108	109	112	112
Carcase meat	g	413	357	235	235	229	230
Other meat and meat products	g	642	712	751	779	803	809
Fish	g	128	140	147	144	157	154
Eggs	no.	3.79	2.88	1.69	1.61	1.65	1.66
Fats	g	315	293	227	193	196	190
Sugar and preserves	g	470	352	212	167	147	146
Fresh potatoes	g	1257	1175	810	727	647	617
Fresh green vegetables	g	341	287	233	246	229	231
Other fresh vegetables	g	405	461	486	506	502	505
Processed vegetables	g	506	625	697	671	620	613
Fresh fruit	g	511	540	693	765	750	794
Processed fruit	g	228	286	375	424	406	413
Bread	g	1029	947	818	782	769	756
Flour	g	156	121	60	69	55	61
Cakes, buns and pastries	g	173	141	173	187	162	163
Biscuits	g	211	198	181	189	166	174
Breakfast cereals	g	82	109	127	135	133	132
Other cereal based products	g	182	190	294	335	371	379
Beverages	g	103	90	74	70	60	58
Other food	g	267	334	498	584	648	667
Soft drinks	ml			1654	1699	1744	1756
Confectionery	g			125	151	128	127
Alcoholic drinks	ml			627	725	735	726

Milk and milk products

UK consumption of all milk and cream has fallen by 33 per cent from 3.0 litres in 1975 to an average of 2.0 litres per person per week in 2002-03. The consumption of liquid whole milk has fallen from over 2.7 litres per person per week in 1975 to 0.6 litres per person per week in 2002-03. The fall in whole milk has been only partly off-set by an increase in other milk and cream. Other milk and cream, of which the main component is skimmed milks, has increased from 0.3 litres to 1.4 litres over the same period with the largest increases in the 1980s. In 2001-02 other milk and cream consumption fell but it has increased again slightly in 2002-03, though remaining below the 2000 level. Chart 2.1 shows the scale of these trends. Cheese consumption has been fairly constant over the same period.

Chart 2.1 Milk Consumption

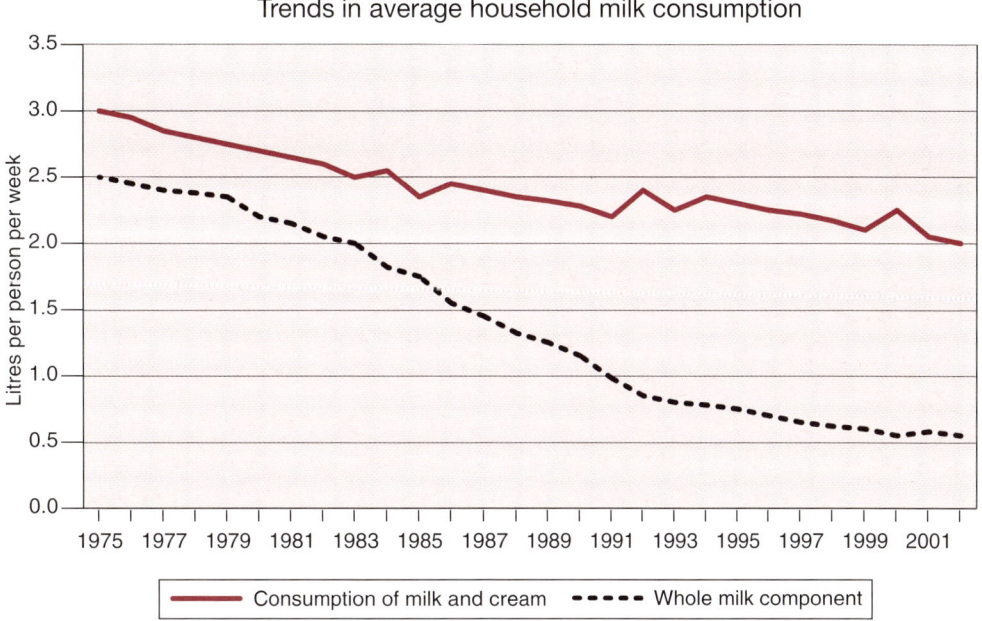

Meat and fish

Carcase meat consumption fell by almost 45 per cent between 1975 and 2002-03 from an average of 413 grams per person per week to 230 grams per person per week. Most of the fall occurred between 1980 and 1995. Since 1995, consumption levels of carcase meat have remained fairly stable. Consumption of non-carcase meat has increased by 26 per cent between 1975 and 2002-03. Consumption of fish has increased by 21 per cent over the same period.

Eggs

Between 1975 and 1999, consumption of eggs declined steadily from an average of 3.8 to 1.6 eggs per person per week. Since 1999, consumption of eggs has increased again slightly to 1.7 eggs per person per week in 2002-03.

Fats and oils and table sugar and preserves

Average consumption of fats and sugar and preserves as measured in the food surveys (see above, excludes fats and sugars in processed foods) have steadily declined since 1975. Fats has declined by 40 per cent between 1975 and 2002-03; sugar and preserves has fallen by 69 per cent over the same period.

Potatoes

Consumption of potatoes has declined between 1975 and 2002-03. Consumption of fresh potatoes has halved between 1975 (1,257 grams per person per week) and 2002-03 (617 grams per person per week). Consumption of processed potatoes, of which the main components are chips and crisps, has doubled over the same period of time.

Chart 2.2 Potato Consumption

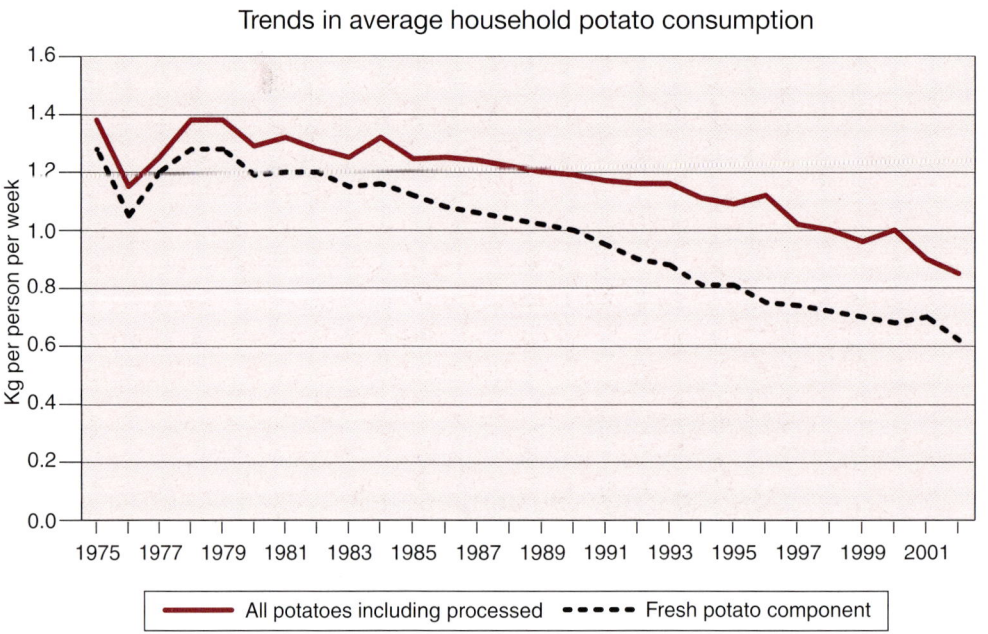

Vegetables

Fresh vegetable consumption has changed little since 1975. However, there has been a shift within the fresh green vegetable category. Average consumption of green fresh vegetables has dropped by 32 per cent from 341 grams per person per week in 1975 to 231 grams per person per week in 2002-03. Over the same period of time, consumption of other fresh vegetables has increased by 25 per cent from 405 to 505 grams per person per week. Consumption of processed vegetables (including processed potatoes) has risen from 506 grams per person per week in 1975 to 613 grams in 2002-03. However, in recent years the trend seems to have been reversed. In 1996 consumption of processed vegetables was highest (727 g); it has decreased steadily since then. Consumption of all vegetables excluding potatoes has increased by 7.7 per cent since 1975.

Fruit

In contrast to vegetable consumption, both fresh fruit and processed fruit consumption has increased between 1975 and 2002-03. Consumption of fresh fruit has increased by 55 per cent from 511 grams per person per week in 1975 to 794 grams per person per week in 2002-03. Bananas account for over 40 per cent of this increase. The 81 per cent increase in processed fruit consumption is almost exclusively driven by an increase in the consumption of fruit juices which more than off-set decreases in canned, dried and frozen fruit.

Bread and cereals

The trend in bread consumption has been downwards since 1975. Between 1975 and 2002-03, consumption of bread has fallen from 1029 to 756 grams per person per week, or by 27 per cent. Flour consumption has dropped by 61 per cent over the same period. This is in line with falling household purchases of fats, oils and table sugar which indicates that more processed and ready to eat food is consumed. Average consumption of cakes, buns and pastries was fairly stable from the mid 1970s to 1990. Between 1990 and 1997 consumption increased reaching its highest point in 1997 at 194 grams per person per week. Since then consumption of cakes, buns and pastries has declined again. Consumption of biscuits and crispbreads has declined fairly steadily since 1975. Consumption of breakfast cereals is 61 per cent higher in 2002-03 than in 1975. Consumption of other cereals, which includes pasta, pizza and rice, has increased from 182 grams per person per week in 1975 to an average of 379 grams per person per week in 2002-03.

Consumption of fruit and vegetables since 1975

Table 2.2 Fruit and vegetable consumption in detail

UK household consumption of fruit and vegetables	1975	Adjusted National Food Survey 1985	1995	2000	Expenditure & Food Survey 2001-02	2002-03	RSE indicator for 2002-03[b]
						grams per person per week	
Fresh potatoes[a]	1257	1175	810	727	647	617	✓✓✓
Processed potatoes[a]	122	166	267	275	260	249	✓✓✓
Fresh green vegetables	341	287	233	246	229	231	✓✓✓
Fresh cauliflower	71	57	78	82	73	76	✓✓✓
Fresh cabbages	136	107	62	51	47	45	✓✓
Lettuce & leafy salads	40	40	56	60	63	61	✓✓
Other fresh green vegetables	94	82	37	53	47	49	
Other fresh vegetables	405	461	486	506	502	505	✓✓✓
Fresh onions, leeks, shallots	85	97	93	98	98	100	✓✓
Fresh carrots	80	114	114	114	102	99	✓✓✓
Fresh tomatoes	112	105	98	98	97	96	✓✓✓
Fresh cucumbers	24	30	35	37	37	37	✓✓
Fresh mushrooms	14	22	36	37	37	35	✓✓✓
Other fresh vegetables	89	93	110	121	131	138	
Fresh fruit	511	540	693	765	750	794	✓✓✓
Fresh bananas	85	83	184	214	203	208	✓✓✓
Fresh apples	198	204	190	187	175	172	✓✓✓
Fresh stone fruit	10	35	39	58	65	72	✓✓
Fresh oranges	100	72	67	55	55	62	✓✓
Fresh grapes	9	18	32	43	49	50	✓✓
Fresh pears	21	31	43	48	39	42	✓✓
Other	88	96	139	159	164	187	
Processed vegetables (exc. Potatoes)	385	459	431	395	360	363	✓✓✓
Frozen vegetables	94	140	166	147	129	130	
Canned baked beans	119	139	129	126	114	111	✓✓✓
Canned vegetables (excl baked beans)	157	165	123	109	104	104	
Other	14	16	13	14	14	18	
Processed fruit	228	286	375	424	406	413	✓✓✓
Pure fruit juices	42	165	272	332	327	333	✓✓✓
Canned fruit	138	76	60	49	40	39	
Other	47	45	43	43	39	41	

(a) excluded from the 5 A DAY statistics
(b) relative standard error. 3 ticks <2.5%, 2 ticks 2.5% – 5%, no ticks indicates "not calculated"

5 A DAY Programme

The 5 A DAY programme is a government initiative to encourage people to eat more fruit and vegetables. Products are individually assessed for inclusion and may then be labelled as part of the programme. It is not practicable within the Expenditure and Food Survey to identify item-by-item those that are within the programme. An approximate approach is used whereby all fruit and vegetables are counted as within the programme except for potatoes.

Fresh green vegetables

UK average consumption of fresh green vegetables has fallen from 341 grams per person per week in 1975 to 231 grams per person per week in 2002-03, a drop of 32 per cent. Consumption of cabbage has fallen by 67 per cent while consumption of cauliflower has remained fairly stable. Average consumption of leafy salads has increased over the same period of time by more than 50 per cent from 40 grams per person per week in

1975 to 61 grams per person per week in 2002-03. Consumption of other fresh green vegetables, of which the largest components are fresh beans and Brussels sprouts, has almost halved between 1975 and 2002-03.

Other fresh vegetables

UK average consumption of onions, carrots and tomatoes are all between 95 and 100 grams per person per week in 2002-03. However, whereas for both onions and carrots consumption is higher in 2002-03 than in 1975, by 17 and 23 per cent respectively, that of tomatoes is 15 per cent lower in 2002-03 compared to 1975. More recently consumption of carrots has declined from an estimated 120 grams per person per week in 1997 to 99 grams per person per week in 2002-03. Consumption of cucumbers has steadily increased since 1975 but the trend seems to have levelled off since 2000. Average consumption of mushrooms in 2002-03 is roughly two and half times higher than in 1975. More recently though consumption levels have been fairly stable.

Fresh fruit

Fresh fruit consumption has increased by 55 per cent between 1975 and 2002-03. Within fresh consumption, consumption has risen for bananas, stone fruit, grapes and pears but has fallen for apples and oranges. On average, consumption of bananas (the largest component of fresh fruit) is just over 200 grams per person per week in 2002-03, up from 85 grams per person per week in 1975. Most of the increase in consumption of bananas has occurred since the mid 1980s. Average consumption of apples has not changed very much even though there is a slow downward trend. Consumption in 2002-03 is 13 per cent lower than in 1975. Average consumption of stone fruit has increased from 10 grams per person per week in 1975 to 72 grams per person per week in 2002-03. Over this period, the trend has always been upwards but since 1995 the rate of increase seems to have accelerated. Of all fresh fruits, oranges are the ones with the highest rate of decline in consumption. Consumption has fallen from 100 grams per person per week in 1975 to 62 grams per person per week in 2002-03 which is a fall of 38 per cent. However, over the last few years, consumption of oranges has increased again from its lowest point in 1999. Average consumption of grapes has increased continuously since 1975 from 9 grams per person per week to 50 grams per person per week in 2002-03. Consumption of pears has doubled between 1975 and 2002-03.

Processed vegetables (excluding potatoes)

Consumption of processed vegetables increased between 1975 and 1985 from 385 grams per person per week to 459 grams per person per week. Since 1985, consumption has been falling. In 2002-03 processed vegetable consumption is estimated at 363 grams per person per week, 5.6 per cent lower than in 1975. Frozen vegetable consumption, the largest component within processed vegetables, increased between 1975 and 1995 but has fallen since then. Average consumption of canned baked beans and canned other vegetables increased between 1975 and 1985 but has fallen since then. Canned baked beans consumption is 6.7 per cent lower in 2002-03 than in 1975; other canned vegetables have fallen by 34 per cent over the same period of time.

Processed Fruit

Processed fruit consumption is estimated to have increased by 81 per cent between 1975 and 2002-03. However, this overall increasing trends masks opposing trends in the two major components of this category. Consumption of pure fruit juices shows a massive increase from 42 grams per person per week in 1975 to 333 grams per person per week in 2002-03 – an almost eight-fold increase. Consumption of canned fruit has fallen from 138 grams per person per week to 39 grams per person per week over the same period of time.

Intakes from household food and drink since 1975

Table 2.3 shows trends in energy and nutrient intakes for household food and drink since 1975. Estimates including eating out are shown in chapter 1 for 2001-02 and 2002-03. The trends, in particular for energy, added sugars, fat and alcohol, are affected by the inclusion since 1992 of the contributions from alcoholic drinks, confectionery and soft drinks brought into the household.

Table 2.3 Trends in intakes from 1975 to 2002-03

UK intakes from household food and drink [a]

		Adjusted National Food Survey				Expenditure & Food Survey	
		1975[b]	1985[b]	1995	2000	2001-02	2002-03
						Intakes per person per day	
Energy	kcal	2489	2208	2143	2152	2089	2091
	MJ	10.4	9.3	9.0	9.0	8.8	8.8
Total Protein	g	75.1	71.0	68.3	72.0	71.3	71.3
Animal Protein	g	46.3	42.9	41.6	42.9	43.3	43.1
Fat	g	111.7	102.1	89.1	86.2	85.7	85.0
Fatty acids:							
Saturates	g	53.4	43.0	35.5	34.6	33.9	33.6
Mono-unsaturates	g	41.7	37.1	32.8	30.8	30.8	30.6
Poly-unsaturates	g	11.0	14.3	14.9	14.9	15.2	15.0
Cholesterol	mg			239	236	237	235
Carbohydrate[c]	g	313	269	272	277	263	265
Total sugars	g			129	131	122	124
Non-milk extrinsic sugars	g			87	88	81	82
starch	g			143	145	140	141
Fibre[d]	g			12.8	13.9	13.3	13.4
Alcohol	g			5.7	7.2	6.9	6.9
Calcium	mg	1064	897	893	967	933	932
Iron	mg	13.0	11.9	10.8	11.5	11.0	11.1
Zinc	mg			8.2	8.7	8.5	8.5
Magnesium	mg			253	266	257	258
Sodium[e]	g		2.80	2.80	2.90	2.87	2.80
Potassium	g			2.84	3.01	2.88	2.87
Thiamin	mg	1.22	1.41	1.45	1.55	1.49	1.51
Riboflavin	mg	1.90	1.91	1.74	1.93	1.84	1.84
Niacin Equivalent	mg	30.3	28.5	27.8	30.6	30.3	30.4
Vitamin B6	mg			2.1	2.3	2.2	2.2
Vitamin B12	µg			5.1	6.3	5.9	5.8
Folate	µg		245	256	269	256	259
Vitamin C	mg	54	56	63	70	67	68
Vitamin A:							
Retinol	µg	1292	1382	1027	613	509	500
Carotene	µg	2174	2401	1824	1906	1762	1753
Retinol equivalent	µg	1756	1784	1330	931	803	800
Vitamin D	µg	2.84	3.16	3.09	3.43	3.28	3.26
Vitamin E	mg			10.96	11.45	11.32	11.13
						as a percentage of food and drink energy	
Fat	%	40.4	41.6	37.4	36.1	36.9	36.6
Fatty acids:							
Saturates	%	19.3	17.5	14.9	14.5	14.6	14.4
Mono-unsaturates	%	15.1	15.1	13.8	12.9	13.3	13.2
Poly-unsaturates	%	4.0	5.8	6.2	6.3	6.5	6.4
Carbohydrate	%	47.2	45.6	47.7	48.2	47.1	47.5

(a) Contributions from pharmaceutical sources are not recorded by the survey
(b) Estimates prior to 1992 exclude intake from confectionery, soft and alcoholic drinks
(c) Available carbohydrate, calculated as monosaccharide
(d) As non starch polysaccharides
(e) Excludes sodium from table salt

Energy

Average energy intake from household food and drink has shown a long-term decline since 1975 (and before) from 2489 Kcal to 2061 Kcal per person per day in 2002-03. In 1992 the contributions from confectionery, soft drinks and alcoholic drinks brought into the household were added, contributing approximately 170 Kcal. Average energy intake in 2002-03, even with this additional contribution, is 16 per cent lower than that in 1975. As would be expected with a long term decline in energy intake, the intakes of many nutrients have also fallen. Average energy intakes since 1940 are shown in chart 1.2 in Chapter 1.

Protein, fat and cholesterol

Average intakes of protein from household food declined slightly between 1975 and 1985 and remained fairly stable since then. Average intake of protein from household food is 71.3 grams per person per day in 2002-03. Average fat intakes have fallen steadily since 1975 though and are 24 per cent lower in 2002-03 than in 1975 (111.7 grams compared to 85.0 grams per person per day). Intakes of saturated and mono-unsaturated fatty acids have fallen whilst intakes of poly-unsaturated fatty acids have increased.

Average cholesterol intakes have remained fairly stable since 1995 when data was first available and are 235 milligrams per person per day in 2002-03.

Carbohydrate, added sugars and fibre

Average carbohydrate intakes from household food have fallen fairly steadily between 1975 and 1991 from 313 grams per person per day to just over 250 grams per person per day in 1991. Between 1992 and 2000 carbohydrate intake has varied around 270 grams per person per day, not showing a discernible trend in either direction. Between 2000 and 2002-03 it fell by 6.9 per cent to an average of 265 grams per person per day.

Non-milk extrinsic sugars exclude sugars that are embodied within the cellular structure of the foods (apart from those in milk) and are sometimes referred to as added sugars. Average intake of non-milk extrinsic sugars (added sugars) from household food has fallen 5.4 per cent since figures were first available in 1992 and is 82 grams per person per day in 2002-03.

Fibre

Average intake of fibre from household food, expressed as non-starch polysaccharides, has remained fairly steady since 1992 when data was first available, and is 13.4 grams per person per day in 2002-03.

Alcohol

Average intake of alcohol from household food and drink has been available since 1992. Over this period of time intakes have increased steadily. In 2002-03 estimated alcohol intake from household food and drink is 21 per cent higher than in 1995. However, in 2002-03 it is estimated to have fallen very slightly suggesting that the increasing trend may be over. These figures exclude alcohol intakes from alcohol consumed outside the home.

Minerals

Intakes of many minerals have fallen in line with falling energy intake. Calcium intake from household food has declined by 24 per cent between 1975 and 1991. Since 1992, calcium intake levels have varied between 880 and 970 milligrams per person per day with little sign of an increasing or decreasing longer-term trend.

Iron intake from household food has declined by 15 per cent between 1975 and 2002-03 and is an average of 11.1 milligrams per person per day in 2002-03. By contrast, there has been little change in zinc and magnesium intakes since figures were first collected in 1992.

Intakes of potassium and sodium, excluding sodium from table salt, have been relatively stable, that for sodium varying between 2.72 and 2.92 grams per person per day since 1985 when figures were first available.

Vitamins

Of the vitamin intakes from household food few show clear long-term trends. However, since 1975 average intake of vitamin A has fallen whilst average intake of vitamin C has increased. Chart 2.3 shows the decline in intake of vitamin A (retinol equivalents) of 59 per cent since 1976 and that it has continued to decline in recent years to 800 micrograms per person per day in 2002-03 on average. This is partly due to the fall in consumption of liver and also due to reductions in the levels of retinol in liver and milk.

Care must be taken when interpreting the estimates for β carotene. Prior to 1990 there were few data available on the levels of individual carotenoids in foods. At about this time data on individual carotenoids which have a lower activity became available and were incorporated, resulting in an apparent decrease in intake of carotene.

Average vitamin C intake in 2002-03 is 26 per cent higher than in 1975, at 68 milligrams per person per day. This reflects the increased consumption of fruit and fruit juice and also soft drinks, many of which are fortified with vitamin C.

Chart 2.3 Intake of retinol equivalent

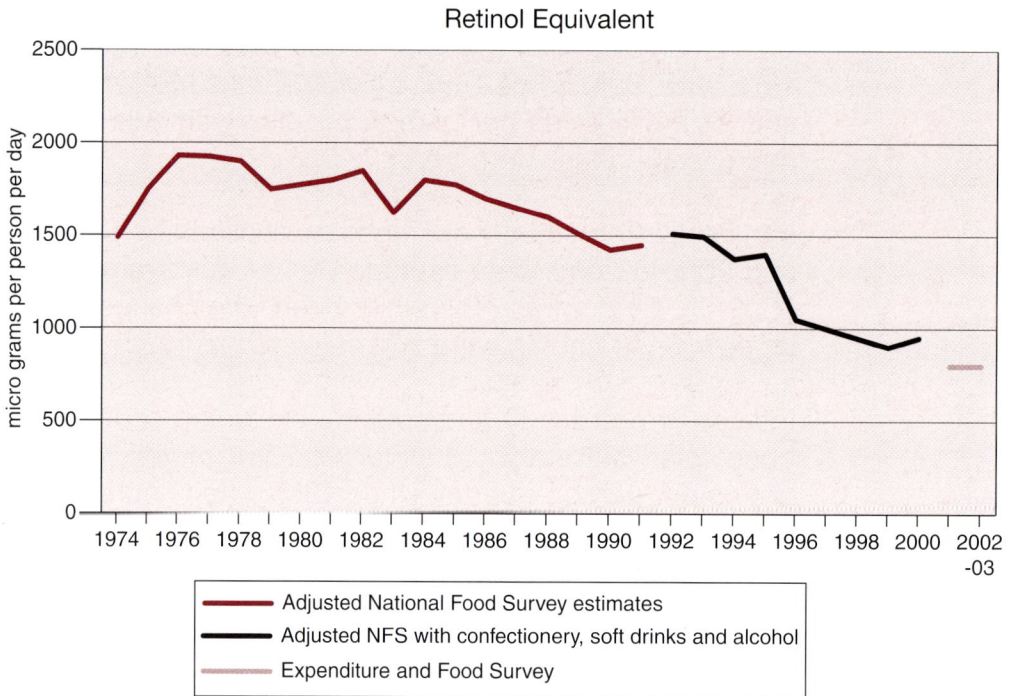

Percentage contributions to energy intake from household food

It is useful to examine the energy obtained from various sources in terms of percentage of total energy intake because it removes the effect of the general reduction in the level of energy intake from household food that has been apparent since the mid sixties – see chart 1.2 in chapter 1.

Table 2.4 shows the percentages of energy derived from fat, from saturated, mono-unsaturated and poly-unsaturated fatty acids and from carbohydrate for household consumption from 1992 to 2002-03.

The estimated average proportions of energy derived from total fat and saturated fatty acids are 36.6 per cent and 14.4 per cent respectively in 2002-03. Both are slightly lower than the corresponding estimates for 2001-02.

The trends since 1992 include confectionery, soft drinks and alcoholic drinks brought into the household. The percentages of energy intake from household food from fat, saturated fatty acids and mono-unsaturated fatty acids have fallen whilst the percentage from poly-unsaturated fatty acids has remained steady.

Table 2.4 Percentage contributions to energy intake since 1992

UK Energy intake from household food and drink[a]

	Energy	Fat	saturated fatty acids	mono-unsaturated fatty acids	poly-unsaturated fatty acids	carbo-hydrate
	kcal	%	%	%	%	%
1992	2225	39.2	15.5	14.5	6.5	46.9
1993	2191	38.7	15.3	14.3	6.4	47.1
1994	2137	38.2	15.0	14.1	6.5	47.4
1995	2143	37.4	14.9	13.8	6.2	47.7
1996	2241	37.5	14.8	13.5	6.6	48.0
1997	2168	37.0	14.7	13.2	6.5	47.9
1998	2102	36.8	14.7	13.1	6.4	47.8
1999	2056	36.2	14.4	12.9	6.4	48.2
2000	2152	36.1	14.5	12.9	6.3	48.2
2001/02	2089	36.9	14.6	13.3	6.5	47.1
2002/03	2091	36.6	14.4	13.2	6.4	47.5

(a) including confectionery, soft drinks and alcoholic drinks brought into the household

Chart 2.4 Percentage energy derived from fat from household consumption

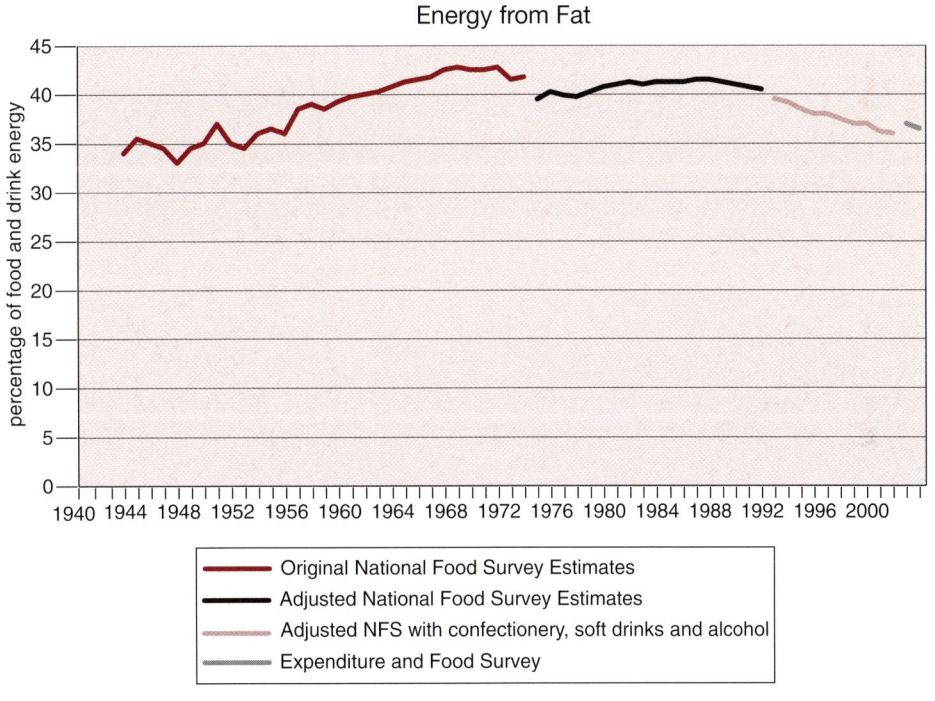

Chart 2.4 shows that the percentage of energy derived from fat in household food increased between 1943 and 1973 from about 35 per cent to 42 per cent. This section of the series is based on original National Food Survey estimates and excludes the contribution from confectionery, soft drinks and alcoholic drinks.

From 1974 the National Food Survey estimates have been adjusted to compensate for under-reporting. Between 1974 and 1991 the original National Food Survey estimated that the percentage of energy derived from fat rose very slightly from 40 per cent to 41 per cent.

From 1992 the estimates include the contribution from confectionery, soft drinks and alcoholic drinks. During the period from 1992 to 2000 the percentage of energy derived from fat fell steadily from 39 per cent to 36 per cent.

The latest estimates, now based on the Expenditure and Food Survey since 2001-02, show a small increase between 2001-02 and 2002-03. An estimated 36.9 per cent of energy from household food and drink was derived from fat in 2001-02, falling to 36.6 per cent in 2002-03.

Chapter 3: Trends in expenditure on food and drink

The figures in this section are based on adjusted NFS results up to 2000 and EFS results from 2001-02 onwards. For more detail on how the adjustments to the NFS results were carried out see chapter 9 of this report.

More detailed series for all years from 1974 to 2002-03 can be found on the Defra website at: http://statistics.defra.gov.uk/esg/publications/efs/default.asp.

Expenditure from 1975 to 2002-03

Table 3.1 shows the trend in UK expenditure in current prices. Changes in expenditure on food and drink in current prices include both changes due to inflation and those due to changes in real expenditure.

Eating out data are only available from 1994 onwards. Data for food and drink eaten out are based on the National Food Survey and are considered less reliable than data based on the Expenditure and Food Survey (2001-02 onwards). This is especially true for data on alcohol consumed outside the home.

Table 3.1 Trends in expenditure

Trends in UK Expenditure on Food and Drink in Current Prices

	1975[a][c]	1985[a][c]	1995[b]	2000[b]	2001-02	2002-03
					£ per person per week	
household food and drink			18.44	20.83	21.52	21.91
food and drink eaten out			5.83[d]	7.36[d]	10.68	10.94
all food and drink			24.27	28.19	32.21	32.85
household food & drink exc. alcohol	4.03	9.91	16.64	18.44	19.08	19.42
food and drink eaten out exc. alcohol			4.31[d]	5.7[d]	6.98	7.21
% eaten out			21%	24%	27%	27%
household alcoholic drink			1.80	2.39	2.44	2.49
eaten out alcoholic drink			1.52[d]	1.66[d]	3.71	3.73
% eaten out			46%	41%	60%	60%

(a) Great Britain only
(b) Estimates on eating out in 1995 and 2000 are based on NFS which was considered less reliable.
(c) Excludes confectionery, soft and alcoholic drinks.
(d) Whilst NFS household food consumption was adjusted, eating out figures were not adjusted.

The table shows that expenditure on alcoholic drinks increased at a higher rate than expenditure on other food and drink.

Expenditure in real terms

Table 3.2 shows expenditure on food and drink in real terms from 1975 to 2002-03. The figures have been derived by deflating expenditure in current prices by the Retail Price Index. The figures do not represent a volume index for which the expenditure figures would have to be deflated using a price index for food only.

Table 3.2 Trends in expenditure in real terms

Trends in UK Expenditure on Food and Drink in Real Terms

£ per person per week	1975[a][c]	1985[a][c]	1995[b]	2000[b]	2001-02	2002-03
						£ per person per week
retail price index	100	277	436	498	508	519
household food and drink			21.95	21.72	21.97	21.91
food and drink eaten out			6.94[d]	7.67[d]	10.91	10.94
all food and drink			28.89	29.39	32.88	32.85
household food & drink exc. alcohol	20.94	18.59	19.81	19.22	19.48	19.42
food and drink eaten out exc. alcohol			5.13[d]	5.94[d]	7.12	7.21
% eaten out			21%	24%	27%	27%
household alcoholic drink			2.14	2.49	2.49	2.49
eaten out alcoholic drink			1.81[d]	1.73[d]	3.78	3.73
% eaten out			46%	41%	60%	60%

(a) Great Britain only
(b) Estimates on eating out in 1995 and 2000 are based on NFS which was considered less reliable.
(c) Excludes confectionery, soft and alcoholic drinks.
(d) Whilst NFS household food consumption was adjusted, eating out figures were not adjusted.

Figures for expenditure on all food and drink are not available for 1975 and 1985 because food eaten out was not collected in the National Food Survey before 1994.

Expenditure on all food and drink increased by 14 per cent between 1995 and 2002-03. However, within all food and drink, different trends are apparent. In real terms, expenditure on food and drink brought home has changed very little between 1995 and 2002-03. The increasing overall trend is due to a large rise in expenditure on food and drink eaten out. Expenditure on food and drink eaten out increased by 58 per cent between 1995 and 2002-03 or from £6.94 per person per week in 1995 to £10.94 in 2002-03.

Figures for expenditure on household food and drink excluding alcohol also exclude confectionery and soft drinks in 1975 and 1985. In real terms, expenditure on household food fell by 7.2 per cent from £20.94 per person per week in 1975 to £19.42 in 2002-03. Between 1995 and 2002-03 expenditure fell by 2.0 per cent. By contrast, expenditure on food and drink eaten out (excluding alcohol) increased by 41 per cent from £5.13 in 1995 to £7.21 in 2002-03.

In real terms, expenditure on alcoholic drinks increased between 1995 and 2002-03 both on alcoholic drinks brought home and those consumed outside the home. Expenditure on alcoholic drinks brought home increased by 16 per cent from £2.14 in 1995 to £2.49 in 2002-03. The figures show a large increase in expenditure on alcoholic drinks consumed outside the home between 2000 and 2001-02. The apparent increase is not reliable though since the National Food Survey eating out results for alcohol are thought to have under-recorded true expenditure.

The percentage of total expenditure, excluding that on alcoholic drinks, spent on eating out is 27 per cent in both 2001-02 and 2002-03. As for alcoholic drinks compared to other food and drink, a higher percentage of expenditure is on consumption outside the home. In 2002-03 60 per cent of all expenditure on alcoholic drinks is for alcoholic drinks consumed outside the home. This is slightly lower than in 2001-02.

Prices

Chart 3.1 Prices since 1975

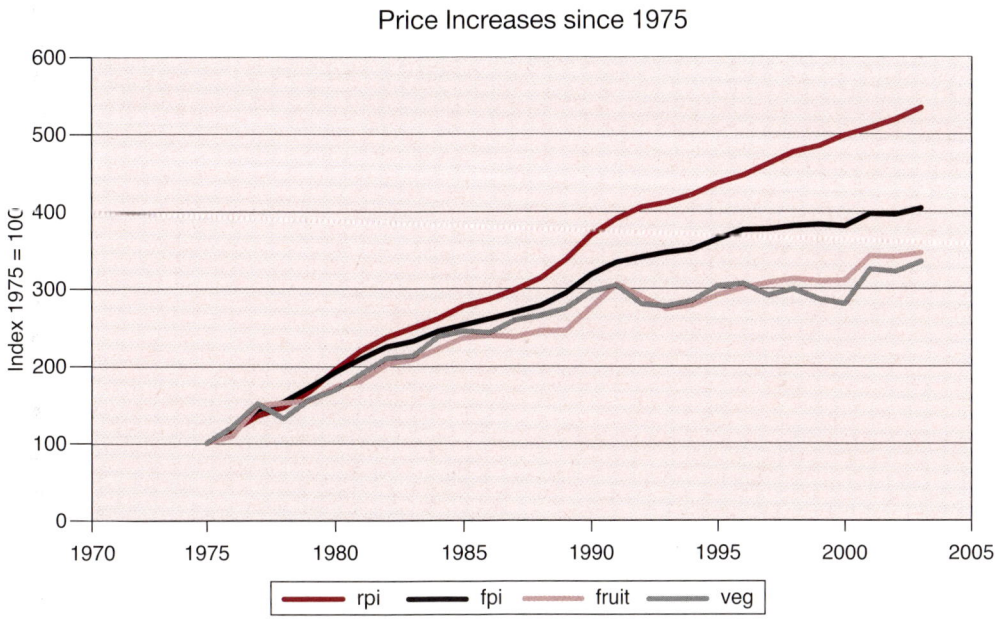

Food prices have lagged behind the Retail Price Index and fruit and vegetable prices have lagged behind the overall food price index. In 2001-02 there was an unusual rise in the price of fruit and vegetables which may explain the estimated drop in consumption that year. Fruit prices rose 10 per cent and vegetable prices 16 per cent. In 2002-03 the prices do not drop back but remain stable. The impact of 2003-04 prices, which rose slightly for fruit and vegetables will be reflected in next year's survey results.

Table 3.3 Price Indices since 2000

Price indices 2000=100	retail price index	food price index	fruit price index	vegetables price index
2000	100	100	100	100
2001-02	102	104	110	116
2002-03	104	104	110	115
2003-04	107	106	112	120

Chapter 4: Food eaten out

The tables in this section show more detailed information on food and drink consumed outside the home for the two years for which more reliable data based on the Expenditure and Food Survey are available. These estimates are incorporated into the figures reported in chapters 1, 3, 6 and 7.

Further estimates are available from the National Food Survey from 1994 to 2000 but these are considered to be of lower quality due to problems with data collection. These data are still of value at aggregated levels and as an indication of trends over time. They have been used in table 4.2 to compile estimates of energy, fat and added sugars from eating out.

Main changes in eating out consumption in 2002-03

- alcoholic drinks −4.0 per cent
- beverages −5.0 per cent
- fish and fish products −4.5 per cent
- potatoes −3.3 per cent
- cheese and egg dishes and pizza +3.9 per cent
- salads +3.5 per cent

Eating out consumption in 2002-03

Table 4.1 shows eating out consumption by type of food. Average UK consumption of alcoholic drinks outside the home is estimated at an average of just over 700 millilitres per person per week in 2002-03. This represents a 4.0 per cent drop compared to the previous year. There is an associated 3.8 per cent drop in intake of alcohol – see Table 4.3. Consumption of soft drinks outside the home is substantially lower than consumption of alcoholic drinks in both years. Soft drink consumption outside the home is broadly unchanged at an average of 376 millilitres per person per week in 2002-03. By contrast, beverages, mainly tea and coffee, have fallen by 5.0 per cent over the same period from 154 millilitres in 2001-02 to 147 millilitres per person per week in 2002-03.

Consumption of meat and meat products eaten out has increased slightly between 2001-02 and 2002-03 from 94 grams to 95 grams. Consumption of potatoes eaten out has fallen by 3.3 per cent over the same period from 88 to 85 grams per person per week. Consumption of sandwiches is slightly increased. In 2002-03, on average 80 grams of sandwiches are consumed per person per week.

The largest increases in consumption between 2001-02 and 2002-03 were for cheese and egg dishes and pizza at +3.9 per cent and for salads at +3.5 per cent. The largest declines in consumption (apart from those for alcoholic drinks and beverages) were recorded for fish and fish products at -4.5 per cent, and for potatoes at -3.3 per cent.

Table 4.1 Eating out consumption in 2002-03

UK average consumption of food and drink eaten out		2001-02	2002-03	% change
		grams per person per week unless otherwise stated		
Alcoholic drinks[a]	ml	732	702	−4.0
Soft drinks inc. milk drinks	ml	373	376	+0.8
Beverages	ml	154	147	−5.0
Meat and meat products		94	95	+0.9
Potatoes		88	85	−3.3
Sandwiches		80	80	+0.6
Vegetables		34	34	+1.9
Ice cream, desserts and cakes		31	32	+2.1
Cheese and egg dishes and pizza		25	26	+3.9
Confectionery		23	22	−2.3
Italian, Indian, Chinese meals		22	22	+1.9
Salads		16	17	+3.5
Rice, pasta and noodles		15	15	−1.9
Other food products		14	14	+2.6
Fish and fish products		15	14	−4.5
Crisps, nuts and snacks		13	12	−2.6
Soups		10	11	na
Bread		9.1	9.2	na
Fruit		8.6	8.4	na
Biscuits		3.7	3.4	na
Yoghurt		2.9	3.3	na
Breakfast cereals		0.2	0.2	na

(a) Assuming consumption is only by over thirteens average consumption of alcoholic drinks in 2002-03 would be 850ml per person over thirteen per week
na – not statistically reliable

Intakes from eating out since 1994

Table 4.2 shows intakes of energy, fat and non-milk extrinsic sugars (added sugars) from household food and food eaten out. Figures from 1994 to 2000 are based on the National Food Survey. Eating out figures from 1994 to 2000 are considered to be of poor quality due to problems with data collection. These data are still of value at aggregated levels and as an indication of trends over time.

The annual change between 2000 and 2001-02 is less reliable than annual changes for other years due to the change in data source, particularly for eating out. The results for household food were adjusted to be broadly comparable to the latest results based on the Expenditure and Food Survey but the results for eating out were not adjusted.

Energy intake from food and drink consumed outside the home is lower in 2002-03 than in 1994 but no clear trend is discernible. Estimates of energy intake from eating out are lower in the Expenditure and Food Survey than in the National Food Survey probably due to the change in data source.

Eating out accounts for 9.1 per cent of energy intake in 2002-03. The apparent drop from 9.7 per cent in 2000 is probably due to the break in the series for eating out. Going back to 1994 10.5 per cent of energy was derived from eating out and this rose to 11.0 per cent in 1999 before falling to current levels. However, it is not clear that there is a downward trend since 1999.

Whilst in aggregate form food eaten out has accounted for between 9.1 per cent and 11.0 per cent of energy intake from food and drink in each of the years since 1994, there are changing patterns in the nature of food eaten out. For example there are more occasions of food eaten out at fast food outlets.

Fat intakes from both household food and drink and food and drink consumed outside the home have been declining. Estimates of fat intake from eating out are lower in the Expenditure and Food Survey than in the National Food Survey (which is consistent with energy intake). Eating out now accounts for 8.5 per cent of fat intake. The apparent drop from 10.4 per cent in 2000 is due to the break in the eating out series.

Compared to 1994, eating out intakes of non-milk extrinsic sugars (added sugars) are higher both in 2000, the last year when NFS was run, and in 2002-03. However, estimates vary substantially from year to year without clear trend.

Table 4.2 Eating out contributions to selected intakes since 1994

Eating out contributions to selected intakes since 1994 in the UK[a]

		from National Food Survey							from Expenditure and Food Survey	
		1994	1995	1996	1997	1998	1999	2000	2001-02	2002-03
averages per person per day										
Energy										
eating out	kcal	250	240	255	265	260	255	230	212	210
household	kcal	2137	2143	2241	2168	2102	2056	2152	2089	2091
% from eating out	%	10.5	10.1	10.2	10.9	11.0	11.0	9.7	9.2	9.1
Fat										
eating out	g	12	11	11	12	12	11	10	8	0
household	g	91	89	93	89	86	83	86	86	85
% from eating out	%	11.7	11.0	10.5	11.9	12.3	11.7	10.4	8.4	8.5
Saturated fatty acids										
eating out	g	4.6	4.4	4.5	4.5	4.5	4.5	4.0	2.8	2.8
household	g	36	36	37	35	34	33	35	33.9	33.6
% from eating out	%	11.4	11.0	10.9	11.3	11.6	12.0	10.4	7.6	7.7
Non-milk extrinsic sugars										
eating out	g	9	9.2	11	11	11	10	10	11	10
household	g	87	87	91	88	84	82	88	81	82
% from eating out	%	9.4	9.6	10.7	11.1	11.6	10.9	10.2	11.6	11.3
Alcohol										
eating out[b]	g	2.9	2.9	2.8	2.9	2.6	2.4	2.3	4.3	4.1
household	g	5.1	5.7	6.0	6.0	6.0	6.3	7.2	6.9	6.9
% from eating out	%	36.5	33.7	31.9	32.6	30.1	27.6	24.2	38.0	37.2

(a) Household estimates have been adjusted to be comparable across the two surveys but eating out estimates have not been adjusted.
(b) Consumption of alcoholic drinks outside the home was severely under-reported in the National Food Survey.

Eating out intakes in 2002-03

Table 4.3 shows how nutrient intakes from food and drink eaten out have changed in the last year. Average intakes of energy and most nutrients have remained fairly constant. Changes in intakes of vitamin C and vitamin A (β carotene and retinol equivalents) from eating out in 2002-03 are due to code changes.

The percentage of energy, excluding energy from alcohol, derived from fat from food eaten out is slightly higher in 2002-03 at 39.3 per cent. This is significantly higher than the 37.4 per cent based on household consumption.

Table 4.3 Eating out energy and nutrient intakes 2001-02 and 2002-03

UK energy and nutrient intakes from food and drink eaten out[a]		2001-02	2002-03	% change
		\multicolumn{3}{c}{average intake per person per day}		
Energy	kcal	212	210	−0.7
	MJ	0.89	0.88	−0.7
Total Protein	g	6.2	6.2	+0.0
Fat	g	7.9	7.9	+0.4
Fatty acids				
Saturates	g	2.8	2.8	+0.5
Mono-unsaturates	g	3.0	3.1	+0.4
Poly-unsaturates	g	1.5	1.5	+0.2
Cholesterol	mg	23.9	24.5	+2.5
Carbohydrate[b]	g	23.0	22.8	−0.9
Total sugars	g	12.3	12.1	−1.6
Non-milk extrinsic sugars	g	10.6	10.5	−0.9
Starch	g	10.7	10.7	−0.2
Fibre[c]	g	0.96	0.94	−1.5
Alcohol	g	4.3	4.1	−3.8
Calcium	mg	62	62	−0.5
Iron	mg	0.80	0.80	+0.7
Zinc	mg	0.70	0.71	+0.8
Magnesium	mg	25	24	−2.4
Sodium[d]	g	0.22	0.23	+3.8
Potassium	g	0.27	0.26	−2.4
Thiamin	mg	0.12	0.12	−0.6
Riboflavin	mg	0.13	0.12	−1.1
Niacin equivalent	mg	3.5	3.5	−0.9
Vitamin B6	mg	0.27	0.26	−3.4
Vitamin B12	µg	0.40	0.41	+2.3
Folate	µg	30	29	−2.3
Vitamin C[e]	mg	6.3	5.2	−17.9
Vitamin A				
Retinol	µg	31	33	+6.9
β-Carotene[e]	µg	187	141	−24.7
Total (retinol equivalent)[e]	µg	62	57	−8.9
Vitamin D	µg	0.24	0.24	+2.7
Vitamin E	mg	1.20	1.19	−1.2
		\multicolumn{3}{c}{contributions to all energy from food & drink excluding alcohol}		
Fat		39.1	39.3	+0.6
Fatty acids				
Saturates	%	13.7	13.8	+0.7
Mono-unsaturates	%	15.1	15.2	+0.5
Poly-unsaturates	%	7.5	7.6	+0.4
Carbohydrate	%	47.5	47.1	−0.7
		\multicolumn{3}{c}{contributions to all energy from food & drink}		
Fat	%	33.6	33.9	+1.1
Fatty acids				
Saturates	%	11.8	11.9	+1.2
Mono-unsaturates	%	12.9	13.1	+1.1
Poly-unsaturates	%	6.5	6.5	+0.9
Carbohydrate	%	40.8	40.7	−0.2

(a) Contributions from pharmaceutical sources are not recorded by the Survey
(b) Available carbohydrate, calculated as monosaccharide
(c) As non-starch polysaccharides
(d) Excludes sodium from table salt
(e) Reported drop is due to code changes

Chapter 5: Household consumption in 2002-03

This Section presents recent trends in consumption and expenditure for food brought into the home for households in the United Kingdom. Consumption of food is based upon expenditure and assumes no waste. The weight of food is measured as it enters the household, not at the point of consumption.

Headline changes

- Milk consumption continues to fall
- Potato consumption, both fresh and processed, is down
- Fruit consumption is up
- Pasta consumption is down after increases each year since 1997
- Mineral water consumption is up
- Alcoholic drink consumption is down slightly

Milk, cream and cheese

Household consumption of milk and cream is 1.6 per cent lower in 2002-03 than in the previous year. Wholemilk consumption continues to decline more sharply than other milks and is now 20 per cent lower than in 1997. Only fully-skimmed milk has risen in consumption, rising by 3.8 per cent whilst semi-skimmed milk has fallen by an estimated 1.3 per cent. The growth areas are in yoghurt and fromage frais and other milks and dairy desserts, with rises of an estimated 6.0 per cent and 4.7 per cent respectively. Cream and cheese consumption remains at previous levels.

Table 5.1 UK consumption and expenditure for milk, cream and cheese

		Consumption			Expenditure		
		1997	2001-02	2002-03	1997	2001-02	2002-03
		millitres per person per week [a]			pence per person per week		
Total milk and cream		2173	2023	1990	147.6	143.9	147.3
Liquid wholemilk, full price		697	598	555	35.8	30.2	28.9
Skimmed milks:		1159	1091	1085	58.7	53.9	55.1
Fully-skimmed		159	160	166	7.6	7.4	7.9
Semi and other skimmed		1000	931	919	51.1	46.4	47.2
Other milks and dairy desserts [b]	(eq ml)	122	160	167	16.4	23.1	24.5
Yoghurt and fromage frais		146	154	163	30.6	31.5	33.5
Cream		20	20	20	5.6	5.3	5.3
Total cheese	(g)	108	112	112	54.5	56.8	57.9
Natural cheese	(g)	97	100	99	49.0	50.3	51.4
Processed cheese	(g)	11	12	12	5.6	6.5	6.6

(a) Except where otherwise stated
(b) Includes condensed, infant and instant milks

Meat, fish and eggs

Household consumption of beef and veal, lamb and mutton and pork remains unchanged in 2002-03. Uncooked poultry consumption has fallen by 3.3 per cent. Other meats show moderate changes in consumption. Home consumption of meat-based ready meals including takeaways continues to rise, showing a year-on-year increase of 8.4 per cent.

There is a modest fall in overall fish consumption. Fresh, chilled or frozen whitefish consumption continues to decline and shows a year-on-year decrease of 8.0 per cent but this is in part countered by a rise in the home consumption of fish ready meals of 6.1 per cent.

Consumption of eggs shows little change in 2002-03, at an average of 1.66 eggs per person per week.

Table 5.2 UK consumption and expenditure for meat, fish and eggs

	Consumption			Expenditure		
	1997	2001-02	2002-03	1997	2001-02	2002-03
	grams per person per week[a]			*pence per person per week*		
Total meat and meat products	983	1032	1039	433.6	458.3	470.4
Carcase	231	229	230	104.8	103.4	106.3
Beef and veal	101	118	118	50.0	56.0	57.2
Mutton and lamb	55	51	51	25.9	23.7	24.8
Pork	74	61	61	28.9	23.7	24.3
Non-carcase	752	803	809	328.8	354.9	364.1
Bacon and ham, uncooked	71	68	69	35.6	36.6	36.4
Bacon and ham, cooked[b]	39	45	45	24.8	31.3	31.2
Poultry, uncooked	197	206	199	61.6	63.0	62.8
Poultry, cooked[c]	36	43	44	19.7	23.5	23.9
Ready meals	117	145	157	53.5	64.5	70.7
Other	292	296	295	133.6	136.0	139.0
Total fish	149	157	154	77.2	92.7	92.8
White, fcf[d][e]	37	36	33	18.5	20.8	19.9
Herrings & other blue fish, fcf[d]	5	6	6	2.5	3.8	3.2
Salmon, fcf[d][e]	8	9	9	4.5	6.9	6.8
Blue fish, dss[f]	4	5	5	3.1	4.1	4.5
White fish, dss[f]	6	4	4	3.0	2.6	2.6
Shellfish	7	10	11	5.4	8.4	9.0
Takeaway fish	11	11	10	8.0	12.9	12.5
Salmon, canned	8	6	6	3.6	3.4	3.0
Other canned or bottled fish	23	29	29	6.7	9.1	9.1
Ready meals	28	36	38	11.1	15.7	17.4
Takeaway fish meals	14	4	4	10.9	5.0	4.8
Eggs (no)	1.64	1.65	1.66	17.7	16.7	17.2

(a) Except where otherwise stated
(b) Includes canned
(c) Excludes canned
(d) Fresh, chilled and frozen
(e) Salmon was included in white fish in 1996-97
(f) Dried, salted and smoked

Fats

Household consumption of total fats and oils has fallen in 2002-03 by 3.2 per cent. Low-fat and reduced-fat spreads have fallen by an estimated 3.5 per cent on the previous year.

Table 5.3 UK Consumption and expenditure for fats and oils

		Consumption			Expenditure	
	1997	2001-02	2002-03	1997	2001-02	2002-03
	grams per person per week[a]			*pence per person per week*		
Total fats and oils	210	196	190	38.4	36.3	36.7
Butter	36	41	37	11.1	11.5	11.0
Margarine	27	13	13	3.0	1.5	1.6
Low fat and reduced fat spreads	79	72	70	14.8	13.8	13.9
Reduced fat spreads	57	58	55	10.8	10.7	10.5
Low fat spreads	22	14	15	4.0	3.0	3.4
Vegetable and salad oils (ml)	52	58	56	6.9	7.1	7.5
Other fats and oils (including lard)	16	13	14	2.7	2.4	2.8

(a) Except where otherwise stated

Sugar and preserves

Consumption of sugar and preserves in 2002-03 shows no significant change on the previous year.

Table 5.4 UK consumption and expenditure for sugar and preserves

	Consumption			Expenditure		
	1997	2001-02	2002-03	1997	2001-02	2002-03
	grams per person per week			*pence per person per week*		
Total sugar and preserves	202	147	146	21.2	15.5	16.1
Sugar	157	112	111	11.8	7.4	7.6
Honey, preserves, syrup & treacle	45	35	35	9.4	8.1	8.5

Fruit and vegetables

There is a decline of 1.7 per cent in the household consumption of all vegetables in 2002-03. However, this is due to the continuing decline of over 4 per cent this year in the consumption of potatoes (both fresh and processed). Overall, the consumption of fresh vegetables excluding potatoes is showing a modest increase. The consumption of canned vegetables is also higher than in the previous year.

Fruit consumption has risen by 4.3% overall in 2002-03. This is driven by rising consumption of fresh fruits, particularly citrus, stone fruits and berry fruits, whilst consumption of apples continues to decline and has fallen by 1.4 per cent compared to the previous year.

Table 5.5 UK consumption and expenditure for vegetables and fruit

	Consumption			Expenditure		
	1997	2001-02	2002-03	1997	2001-02	2002-03
	grams per person per week[a]			*pence per person per week*		
Total vegetables	2235	1999	1965	252.2	271.0	268.9
Fresh potatoes	764	647	617	26.0	35.7	31.0
Fresh green vegetables	257	229	231	31.4	39.6	40.2
Fresh cabbages	62	47	45	4.1	4.3	4.2
Fresh cauliflowers	87	73	76	8.8	8.9	8.8
Other fresh vegetables	512	502	505	60.1	75.5	77.0
Fresh carrots	120	102	99	6.2	6.8	6.3
Onions, leeks & shallots	99	98	100	8.7	10.5	10.8
Fresh tomatoes	100	97	96	12.4	16.6	17.7
Miscellaneous other fresh	65	83	86	14.2	21.2	22.1
Processed potatoes	277	260	249	73.9	68.3	67.6
All frozen vegetables[b]	105	71	71	17.3	9.9	9.7
Other vegetables, not frozen[c]	319	289	292	43.5	42.1	43.4
Total fruit	1132	1156	1206	133.8	149.5	159.3
Fresh fruit	731	750	794	89.0	101.9	110.5
Fresh apples	186	175	172	20.2	19.3	20.8
Fresh bananas	203	203	208	20.3	21.9	20.9
Fruit juices (ml)	301	327	333	23.6	26.7	27.1
Other fruit products	100	79	80	21.2	20.9	21.7

(a) Except where otherwise stated
(b) Excludes frozen potato products
(c) Mainly processed tomatoes, peas & beans and ready meals

Bread, cereals and cereal products

Overall, there is little change in household bread consumption in 2002-03. In the loaf sector, white bread consumption has decreased by 5.3 per cent, wholemeal consumption by 4.9 per cent, whilst brown bread consumption has reversed last year's fall and risen by 28 per cent. There is a rise in the home consumption of rolls and sandwiches of 2.8 per cent and in other breads of 5.1 per cent. Flour consumption has risen by 13 per cent in 2002-03, not quite reversing the previous year's fall, and bun, scone and teacake consumption has risen by 13 per cent. Rice consumption is up by 6.8 per cent whilst pasta and pizza consumption are down by 1.4 per cent and 4.1 per cent respectively. Despite this year's fall, pasta consumption has increased 173 per cent since 1997. Household consumption of breakfast cereals remains static.

Table 5.6 UK consumption and expenditure for bread, cereals and cereal products

	Consumption			Expenditure		
	1997	2001-02	2002-03	1997	2001-02	2002-03
	grams per person per week			*pence per person per week*		
Total cereals including bread	1708	1655	1665	321.1	357.5	366.4
Bread	810	769	756	78.9	86.2	88.3
White bread	469	456	431	31.1	32.4	32.4
Brown bread	86	36	46	7.4	3.2	4.2
Wholemeal bread	98	106	100	8.0	9.2	8.9
Rolls and sandwiches	83	86	88	17.7	21.3	21.9
Other bread	80	94	99	18.4	25.9	27.1
Cereals excluding bread	898	886	909	242.2	271.2	278.1
Flour	56	55	61	2.2	2.4	2.8
Cakes and pastries	163	139	133	54.4	50.3	51.0
Buns, scones and tea-cakes	49	37	41	10.6	8.2	9.5
Biscuits	185	166	174	51.1	48.9	53.8
Oatmeal and oat products	15	12	13	1.7	1.6	1.9
Breakfast cereals	127	133	132	33.7	35.3	35.9
Rice	82	76	81	16.2	21.7	21.6
Pasta	32	89	88	2.9	14.9	14.5
Pizza	57	67	65	29.4	44.4	41.0
Other cereals	130	113	121	39.9	43.7	46.0

Beverages and miscellaneous foods

There is no significant change in the consumption of beverages in the home in 2002-03. Consumption of mineral water continues to rise with a year-on-year increase of 6.8 per cent and a five year increase of 22 per cent.

Table 5.7 UK consumption and expenditure for beverages and miscellaneous foods

		Consumption			Expenditure		
		1997	2001-02	2002-03	1997	2001-02	2002-03
		grams per person per week[a]			pence per person per week		
Total beverages		71	60	58	51.1	43.8	42.2
Tea		39	34	34	19.1	17.8	17.9
Coffee		16	16	16	24.0	21.8	20.6
Cocoa and drinking chocolate		7	5	4	3.0	2.5	2.2
Branded food drinks		9	4	4	5.0	1.7	1.5
Total miscellaneous		538	648	667	95.0	113.2	116.2
Mineral water	(ml)	172	197	210	7.2	7.6	8.0
Soups		74	83	83	11.3	12.9	13.3
Pickles and sauces		109	121	123	26.1	31.6	32.1
Ice-cream & ice-cream products	(ml)	126	182	185	19.0	21.8	21.8
Other foods[b]		57	65	66	30.7	39.0	39.9

(a) Except where otherwise stated
(b) Including, salt and other miscellaneous food items

Soft and alcoholic drinks and confectionery

In line with the other results presented in this section, the estimates for drinks and confectionery shown in Table 5.8 refer only to household consumption and exclude those purchases not taken home. Eating out consumption is covered in chapter 4.

In 2002-03 home consumption of ready-to-drink soft drinks has risen by 3.1 per cent whereas consumption of concentrated soft drinks has fallen by 3.4 per cent. Low-calorie concentrated soft drink consumption has risen by 6 per cent. Alcoholic drink consumption has fallen 1.2 per cent in overall terms. The consumption of beer has risen by 3.4 per cent whilst that of lager has fallen 3.4 per cent, resulting in a combined fall in consumption of lager and beer when taken together. Wine consumption remains little changed and all other alcoholic drinks show a fall of 1.4 per cent on the previous year.

Consumption of confectionery fell by less than 1 per cent overall which was mainly due to a fall in the consumption of chocolate confectionery of 2.2 per cent.

Table 5.8 UK consumption and expenditure for drinks and confectionery brought home

	Consumption			Expenditure		
	1997	2001-02	2002-03	1997	2001-02	2002-03
	millilitres per person per week			*pence per person per week*		
Total soft drinks[a]	**1625**	**1744**	**1756**	**57.2**	**72.0**	**74.0**
Concentrated[b]	586	608	587	11.0	10.5	10.3
Ready to drink	522	657	677	27.6	41.5	43.6
Low-calorie, concentrated[b]	235	144	153	4.2	2.6	2.5
Low-calorie, ready to drink	282	335	339	14.5	17.4	17.6
Total alcoholic drinks[d]	**653**	**735**	**726**	**193.4**	**244.2**	**248.8**
Lager and beer[c]	365	386	380	59.7	65.4	64.9
Wine	179	222	220	75.4	106.5	109.9
Other	109	127	125	58.3	72.3	74.0
	grams per person per week			*pence per person per week*		
Total confectionery	**134**	**128**	**127**	**71.8**	**80.8**	**76.6**
Chocolate confectionery	96	85	83	54.2	57.2	52.4
Mints and boiled sweets	32	37	38	14.0	18.7	19.0
Other	6	6	6	3.5	4.9	5.2

(a) Excluding pure fruit juices which are recorded in the survey under fruit products
(b) Converted to unconcentrated equivalent
(c) Including low alcohol lager and beers
(d) Average consumption by population aged 14 years and over was 878 millilitres per person per week

Takeaway foods

Takeaway food consumption has fallen slightly in 2002-03. The highest consumption in this category is of meat-based meals such as Indian and Chinese takeaways, rice, chips and pizza where consumption is estimated to be unchanged in 2002-03. Home consumption of takeaway fish has fallen by 6.7 per cent, although consumption of chips shows an increase of 0.9 per cent.

Table 5.9 UK consumption and expenditure for takeaways

	Consumption		Expenditure	
	2001-02	2002-03	2001-02	2002-03
	grams per person per week		*pence per person per week*	
Total Meat	53	54	61.1	62.5
Chicken	4	5	5.1	5.5
Meat pies & pasties	3	3	2.0	2.1
Burger & bun	6	5	5.7	5.4
Kebabs	7	7	5.9	6.4
Sausages & saveloys	2	2	1.6	2.0
Meat Based meals	31	31	40.6	40.9
Miscellaneous meats	0	0	0.2	0.1
Total Fish	15	14	17.9	17.3
Fish	11	10	12.9	12.5
Fish products	1	0	0.7	0.5
Fish based meals	3	3	4.3	4.3
Total Vegetables	50	49	25.8	24.8
Chips	42	42	18.6	19.0
Vegetable takeaway products	9	7	7.2	5.9
Total Bread	4	3	5.5	5.0
Sandwiches	2	2	2.7	2.4
Breads	1	1	2.8	2.7
Total Other cereals	38	37	38.6	35.7
Pastries	1	1	0.8	1.0
Rice	18	17	13.0	12.5
Pasta & noodles	1	1	0.7	0.9
Pizza	18	17	22.5	19.9
Crisps and other savoury snacks	1	1	1.6	1.5
Total Miscellaneous	2	2	2.6	2.8
Soups	0	0	0.3	0.4
Sauces and mayonnaise	0	0	1.3	1.3
Ice cream & ice cream products	1	1	0.9	1.0
Confectionery	0	0	0.2	0.1

Chapter 6: Regional Comparisons

This section contains comparisons based on the countries and regions of the United Kingdom. Care in interpretation is required because the sampling error below the UK level is higher. The sample size is given at the top of each column as an indication of the reliability of the figures. Differences in relative prices and household income should also be born in mind when interpreting the data.

The consumption and expenditure tables contain data from both household food and drink and eating out. The energy and nutrient intake tables not only include the combined intakes from food brought into the home and eaten out but also the contributions from soft drinks, alcoholic drinks and confectionery.

For a more detailed breakdown of the data, please refer to the datasets which are published on the Defra website at:
http://statistics.defra.gov.uk/esg/publications/efs/default.asp

United Kingdom countries

Household

Tables 6.1 and 6.2 show that, as in 2001-02, there is little variation between the countries in the household consumption of milk and cream, all meat and meat products, total cereals and confectionery with the ratio of consumption in the highest consuming country to consumption in the lowest consuming region being 1.2 or less. Home consumption of fruit and vegetables (excluding potatoes) remains highest in England and lowest in Northern Ireland. The trend in household consumption of fresh potatoes also continues with that in Northern Ireland being over one and a half times more than that in Scotland. Households in England continue to eat most cheese and Northern Ireland households remain the lowest consumers of cheese, fish, sugar and preserves. Scotland households continue to have the highest consumption of soft drinks. A trend may also be emerging in the home consumption of alcoholic drinks with Welsh households remaining the highest consumers and Northern Ireland the lowest whilst household expenditure on alcoholic drinks is again highest in Scotland. Total expenditure on household food and drink varies little between countries.

Eating out

Generally there are wider variations in the consumption of food and drink eaten out with households in Scotland consuming nearly twice as much fish and fish products and sandwiches as households in Northern Ireland. Households in England drink more than one and a half times the amount of beverages outside the home than households in Northern Ireland. The ratio is similar in both the consumption of soft drinks between Scotland and Northern Ireland households and the consumption of alcoholic drinks between households in Wales and Northern Ireland. Expenditure on alcoholic drinks outside the home is highest in England. The levels of consumption in meat and meat products, potatoes and ice cream, cakes and desserts eaten out are similar in all four countries. There is little variation between the countries in expenditure on food and drink eaten outside the home, which generally represents around one third of the overall expenditure on food and drink.

Intakes

Intakes of energy and nutrients are similar in England, Scotland and Wales, but Northern Ireland households have the lowest intakes overall.

Table 6.1 Highest and lowest consuming countries 2002-03

United Kingdom Countries

	Lowest	Highest	Ratio of lowest to highest
Household Consumption			
Milk and cream	ENGLAND	N. IRELAND	1.1
Cheese	N. IRELAND	ENGLAND	1.6
Carcase meat	SCOTLAND	N. IRELAND	1.2
Other meat and meat products	N. IRELAND	WALES	1.1
Fish	N. IRELAND	ENGLAND	1.5
Fats and oils	SCOTLAND	WALES	1.2
Sugar and preserves	N. IRELAND	WALES	1.4
Potatoes	SCOTLAND	N. IRELAND	1.6
Vegetables	N. IRELAND	ENGLAND	1.4
Fruit	N. IRELAND	ENGLAND	1.4
Total Cereals	WALES	SCOTLAND	1.1
Beverages	N. IRELAND	ENGLAND	1.3
Soft drinks[a]	N. IRELAND	SCOTLAND	1.3
Alcoholic drinks	N. IRELAND	WALES	1.5
Confectionery	ENGLAND	WALES	1.1
Eating Out Consumption			
Ethnic meals	N. IRELAND	ENGLAND	1.3
Meat and meat products	SCOTLAND	N. IRELAND	1.2
Fish and fish products	N. IRELAND	SCOTLAND	1.9
Cheese and egg dishes and pizza	WALES	ENGLAND	1.4
Potatoes	ENGLAND	N. IRELAND	1.2
Vegetables	SCOTLAND	ENGLAND	1.5
Sandwiches	N. IRELAND	SCOTLAND	1.9
Ice creams, desserts and cakes	WALES	SCOTLAND	1.2
Beverages	N. IRELAND	ENGLAND	1.7
Soft drinks including milk	WALES	SCOTLAND	1.5
Alcoholic drinks	N. IRELAND	WALES	1.4
Confectionery	ENGLAND	SCOTLAND	1.4
Household Expenditure			
Total all food & drink excluding alcohol	WALES	SCOTLAND	1.1
Total all food & drink	WALES	SCOTLAND	1.1
Eating Out Expenditure			
Total all food & drink excluding alcohol	WALES	ENGLAND	1.2
Total all food & drink	WALES	ENGLAND	1.1

Table 6.2 Consumption and expenditure of selected foods by country 2002-03

United Kingdom & Countries

		United Kingdom	England	Wales	Scotland	Northern Ireland
Number of households in sample		6927	5400	357	585	585
Average age of HRP		51	52	52	50	50
Average number of adults per household		1.86	1.86	1.75	1.81	1.96
Average number of children per household		0.53	0.53	0.5	0.49	0.65
Average gross weekly household income (£)		539.88	561.74	436.98	492.21	448.45

Household Consumption — *grams per person per week unless otherwise stated*

		UK	England	Wales	Scotland	N. Ireland
Milk and cream	(ml)	1990	1970	2094	2091	2107
Cheese		112	114	100	111	70
Carcase meat		230	232	222	212	246
Other meat and meat products		809	806	841	826	785
Fish		154	158	149	137	105
Eggs	(no.)	1.7	1.7	1.7	1.8	1.5
Fats and oils		190	192	198	160	179
Sugar and preserves		146	148	164	123	115
Potatoes		867	849	997	808	1328
Vegetables		1099	1129	1071	926	787
Fruit		1206	1242	1026	1068	886
Total Cereals		1665	1665	1618	1701	1664
Beverages		58	60	58	48	46
Soft drinks[a]	(ml)	1756	1713	1766	2188	1682
Alcoholic drinks	(ml)	726	737	759	673	500
Confectionery		127	124	142	142	135

Eating Out Consumption — *grams per person per week unless otherwise stated*

		UK	England	Wales	Scotland	N. Ireland
Ethnic meals		22	23	20	21	18
Meat and meat products		95	94	99	92	110
Fish and fish products		14	14	13	15	8
Cheese and egg dishes and pizza		26	27	19	21	20
Potatoes		85	84	89	89	101
Vegetables		34	36	35	23	26
Sandwiches		80	82	55	90	47
Ice creams, desserts and cakes		32	31	28	35	35
Beverages	(ml)	147	153	100	134	88
Soft drinks including milk	(ml)	376	360	354	527	423
Alcoholic drinks	(ml)	702	714	787	590	558
Confectionery		22	21	23	30	28

Household Expenditure — *pence per person per week unless otherwise stated*

	UK	England	Wales	Scotland	N. Ireland
Milk and cream	147.3	147.2	146.7	147.1	151.6
Cheese	57.9	59.2	47.8	58.3	38.8
Carcase meat	106.3	105.7	104.6	105.3	128.8
Other meat and meat products	364.1	360.8	345.2	395.5	397.6
Fish	92.8	95.1	83.3	85.7	63.5
Eggs	17.2	17.4	16.1	17.4	15.5
Fats and oils	36.7	37.1	35.8	34.1	35.5
Sugar and preserves	16.1	16.4	16.1	13.8	13.9
Potatoes	98.6	96.0	102.6	111.2	129.6
Vegetables	170.3	175.1	150.9	149.9	122.6
Fruit	159.3	164.0	137.9	139.8	117.0
Total Cereals	366.4	366.3	321.8	387.9	380.3
Beverages	42.2	43.4	39.2	35.5	32.7
Soft drinks	74.0	70.9	65.4	104.4	85.5
Alcoholic drinks	248.8	250.4	233.6	257.6	202.9
Confectionery	76.6	75.3	83.6	85.7	76.4
Total all food & drink excluding alcohol	1942.1	1946.4	1805.1	1996.6	1892.5
Total all food & drink	2190.9	2196.7	2038.7	2254.2	2095.4

Eating Out Expenditure — *pence per person per week unless otherwise stated*

	UK	England	Wales	Scotland	N. Ireland
Total all food & drink excluding alcohol	721.1	731.4	599.4	704.9	679.8
Total all food & drink	1093.6	1109.0	965.1	1046.9	1006.1

(a) Converted to unconcentrated equivalent by applying a factor of 5 to concentrated and low calorie concentrated soft drinks

Table 6.3 Energy and nutrient intakes from all food and drink by country 2002-03

United Kingdom & Countries		United Kingdom	England	Wales	Scotland	Northern Ireland
Number of households in sample		6927	5400	357	585	585
Average age of HRP		51	52	52	50	50
Average number of adults per household		1.86	1.86	1.75	1.81	1.96
Average number of children per household		0.53	0.53	0.5	0.49	0.65
Average gross weekly household income (£)		539.88	561.74	436.98	492.21	448.45
Total Energy & Nutrient Intakes[a]					*intake per person per day*	
Energy	kcal	2301	2310	2290	2300	2190
	MJ	9.7	9.7	9.6	9.7	9.2
Total Protein	g	77.6	77.7	76.8	77.7	74.9
Fat	g	92.9	93	93	92	88
Fatty acids:						
Saturates	g	36.4	36.3	36.5	37.1	35
Mono-unsaturates	g	33.7	33.8	33.4	32.9	31.9
Poly-unsaturates	g	16.5	16.7	16.4	15.2	14.8
Cholesterol	mg	259	260	258	259	243
Carbohydrate[b]	g	287	288	285	289	279
Total sugars	g	136	136	137	136	126
Non-milk extrinsic sugars	g	92	92	94	94	86
Starch	g	152	151	148	153	153
Fibre[c]	g	14.4	14.5	14.3	13.7	13.5
Alcohol	g	11.0	11.0	11.0	11.0	8.0
Calcium	mg	993	990	1000	1020	960
Iron	mg	11.9	11.9	11.8	11.6	11.2
Zinc	mg	9.2	9.2	9.1	9.2	8.8
Magnesium	mg	282	283	278	277	264
Sodium[d]	g	3.03	3.02	3.04	3.21	2.93
Potassium	g	3.14	3.15	3.13	3.06	3.04
Thiamin	mg	1.63	1.63	1.6	1.62	1.61
Riboflavin	mg	1.97	1.97	1.98	1.95	1.89
Niacin Equivalent	mg	33.9	34	33.4	33.5	32.5
Vitamin B6	mg	2.4	2.4	2.5	2.4	2.5
Vitamin B12	µg	6.2	6.2	6.2	6.4	5.7
Folate	µg	288	290	286	275	273
Vitamin C	mg	74	75	67	71	65
Vitamin A:						
Retinol	µg	533	540	460	520	410
β-carotene	µg	1894	1920	1980	1720	1600
Retinol equivalent	µg	856	870	800	820	680
Vitamin D	µg	3.51	3.53	3.55	3.33	3.26
Vitamin E	mg	12.32	12.47	12.31	11.31	11.01
				as a percentage of total food & drink energy		
Fat	%	36.3	36.4	36.4	35.9	36
Fatty acids:						
Saturates	%	14.2	14.2	14.3	14.5	14.4
Mono-unsaturates	%	13.2	13.2	13.1	12.9	13.1
Poly-unsaturates	%	6.4	6.5	6.5	6.0	6.1
Carbohydrate	%	46.8	46.8	46.7	47.2	47.7

(a) Contributions from pharmaceutical sources are not recorded by the Survey
(b) Available carbohydrate, calculated as monosaccharide
(c) As non-starch polysaccharides
(d) Excludes sodium from table salt

England regions

Household

At the regional level, few year on year trends in levels of consumption and expenditure are emerging (Tables 6.4 and 6.5). Home consumption of milk and cream, non-carcase meat, potatoes, confectionery and all beverages and drinks is lowest in London whereas household consumption of milk and cream, all meat and meat products, beverages and confectionery is highest in the North East. Vegetable (excluding potatoes) and fruit consumption is highest in the East and South West respectively with the lowest consumption levels for both vegetables and fruit being recorded in the North East. Household consumption of alcoholic drinks is highest in the South West but expenditure is highest in the North West. There is little variation in household expenditure on food and drink between the regions.

Eating out

As is to be expected, levels of eating out are highest in London where more than twice as many Indian, Chinese and ethnic-type meals are consumed than in the East Midlands. Amongst London households, one and a half times more cheese and egg dishes and pizza are eaten out than in those in the North West. Consumption of and expenditure on alcoholic drinks outside the home is highest in the North East. For all food and drink outside the home, the ratio of expenditure in London to expenditure in the South West is 1.4. There is a wider variation than at country level in eating out expenditure as a percentage of overall food and drink spending, with 38.4 per cent of the total being spent on eating out in London compared to 28.2 per cent in the South West.

Intakes

Table 6.6 compares the energy and nutrient intakes across the regions. Energy intake and the intakes of most nutrients are highest in the North West and lowest in London. The proportion of total energy obtained from total fat is highest in the North East and lowest in London, whilst the proportion of energy obtained from carbohydrate is lowest in the North East and highest in London. London also has the lowest proportion of total energy derived from saturated fatty acids, and the highest proportion of total energy derived from polyunsaturated fatty acids.

Table 6.4 Highest and lowest consuming regions 2002-03

England Regions	Lowest	Highest	Ratio of lowest to highest
Household Consumption			
Milk and cream	London	North East	1.4
Cheese	North East	South West	1.3
Carcase meat	North West	North East	1.2
Other meat and meat products	London	North East	1.3
Fish	North West	London	1.4
Fats and oils	South East	Yorkshire & the Humber	1.3
Sugar and preserves	South East	West Midlands	1.3
Potatoes	London	West Midlands	1.5
Vegetables	North East	East	1.4
Fruit	North East	South West	1.4
Total Cereals	East	Yorkshire & the Humber	1.1
Beverages	London	North East	1.9
Soft drinks	London	South East	1.4
Alcoholic drinks	London	South West	1.6
Confectionery	London	North East	1.7
Eating Out Consumption			
Ethnic meals	East Midlands	London	2.3
Meat and meat products	West Midlands	North West	1.2
Fish and fish products	West Midlands	Yorkshire & the Humber	1.7
Cheese and egg dishes and pizza	North West	London	1.5
Potatoes	South East	North East	1.4
Vegetables	South East	South West	1.3
Sandwiches	South West	London	1.7
Ice creams, desserts and cakes	West Midlands	London	1.4
Beverages	North East	East Midlands	1.4
Soft drinks including milk	South West	North East	1.7
Alcoholic drinks	East	North East	1.8
Confectionery	East	North East	1.7
Household Expenditure			
Total all food & drink excluding alcohol	West Midlands	South West	1.2
Total all food & drink	West Midlands	South West	1.2
Eating Out Expenditure			
Total all food & drink excluding alcohol	West Midlands	London	1.6
Total all food & drink	South West	London	1.4

Table 6.5 Consumption and expenditure of selected foods by region 2002-03

England & Regions		England	North East	North West	Yorkshire and The Humber	East Midlands
Number of households in sample		5400	318	747	560	438
Average age of HRP		52	51	51	52	51
Average number of adults per household		1.86	1.83	1.88	1.82	1.86
Average number of children per household		0.53	0.61	0.55	0.51	0.59
Average gross weekly household income (£)		561.74	465.17	490.84	472.84	538.49
Household Consumption		*grams per person per week unless otherwise stated*				
Milk and cream	(ml)	1970	2259	2049	2006	2064
Cheese		114	94	104	114	121
Carcase meat		232	251	206	233	225
Other meat and meat products		806	896	873	776	817
Fish		158	138	135	141	154
Eggs	(no.)	1.7	1.5	1.5	1.7	1.6
Fats and oils		192	167	183	211	186
Sugar and preserves		148	135	134	156	157
Potatoes		849	876	837	942	890
Vegetables		1129	876	950	1142	1084
Fruit		1242	1005	1053	1053	1141
Total Cereals		1665	1648	1652	1704	1694
Beverages		60	81	66	66	65
Soft drinks (a)	(ml)	1713	1700	1793	1731	1812
Alcoholic drinks	(ml)	737	804	876	757	796
Confectionery		124	153	141	112	123
Eating Out Consumption		*grams per person per week unless otherwise stated*				
Ethnic meals		23	16	20	25	15
Meat and meat products		95	97	102	95	95
Fish and fish products		14	17	13	19	13
Cheese and egg dishes and pizza		26	31	23	24	25
Potatoes		85	101	89	93	85
Vegetables		34	34	34	39	38
Sandwiches		80	82	90	79	80
Ice creams, desserts and cakes		32	28	30	31	27
Beverages	(ml)	147	134	159	135	192
Soft drinks including milk	(ml)	376	423	399	363	343
Alcoholic drinks	(ml)	702	1007	859	872	727
Confectionery		22	31	26	22	25
Household Expenditure		*pence per person per week unless otherwise stated*				
Milk and cream		147.2	151.5	148.4	142.6	154.3
Cheese		59.2	43.8	50.2	58.4	58.8
Carcase meat		105.7	111.2	96.0	108.5	101.1
Other meat and meat products		360.8	377.9	375.0	347.9	349.1
Fish		95.1	72.2	73.4	76.7	88.0
Eggs		17.4	14.6	15.0	16.8	15.6
Fats and oils		37.1	32.1	35.4	37.5	36.1
Sugar and preserves		16.4	15.0	13.6	15.3	16.7
Potatoes		96.0	99.9	96.4	105.8	102.1
Vegetables		175.1	130.7	141.0	162.1	158.7
Fruit		164.0	123.6	131.2	130.2	144.9
Total Cereals		366.3	334.2	359.6	350.0	362.2
Beverages		43.4	51.0	46.0	45.2	45.6
Soft drinks		70.9	73.0	73.2	68.8	68.4
Alcoholic drinks		250.4	219.2	277.3	249.2	255.4
Confectionery		75.3	97.2	82.0	68.4	77.4
Total all food & drink excluding alcohol		1946.4	1829.9	1845.8	1840.0	1891.4
Total all food & drink		2196.7	2049.1	2123.0	2089.2	2146.8
Eating Out Expenditure		*pence per person per week unless otherwise stated*				
Total all food & drink excluding alcohol		731.4	595.1	622.5	629.5	702.3
Total all food & drink		1109.0	1046.4	1000.9	1059.1	1146.8

(a) Converted to unconcentrated equivalent by applying a factor of 5 to concentrated and low calorie concentrated soft drinks

Table 6.5 continued

England & Regions (continued)		West Midlands	East	London	South East	South West
Number of households in sample		558	638	605	920	616
Average age of HRP		51	51	49.6	51.1	55
Average number of adults per household		1.94	1.85	1.86	1.88	1.83
Average number of children per household		0.55	0.53	0.59	0.53	0.37
Average gross weekly household income (£)		488.63	581.29	771.73	644.65	510.95
Household Consumption		*grams per person per week unless otherwise stated*				
Milk and cream	(ml)	2094	1893	1665	2091	1937
Cheese		100	118	105	111	124
Carcase meat		222	222	229	212	232
Other meat and meat products		841	792	713	826	802
Fish		149	169	184	137	157
Eggs	(no.)	1.7	1.6	1.7	1.8	1.6
Fats and oils		198	173	184	160	191
Sugar and preserves		164	151	131	123	142
Potatoes		997	858	670	808	850
Vegetables		1071	1230	1139	926	1177
Fruit		1026	1383	1376	1068	1386
Total Cereals		1618	1600	1618	1701	1638
Beverages		58	56	42	48	61
Soft drinks[a]	(ml)	1766	1780	1568	2188	1718
Alcoholic drinks	(ml)	759	694	542	673	719
Confectionery		142	130	90	142	126
Eating Out Consumption		*grams per person per week unless otherwise stated*				
Ethnic meals		21	22	35	26	16
Meat and meat products		82	95	100	95	82
Fish and fish products		11	13	16	12	16
Cheese and egg dishes and pizza		26	29	34	25	25
Potatoes		86	85	86	73	74
Vegetables		32	39	35	32	42
Sandwiches		69	78	107	77	64
Ice creams, desserts and cakes		27	31	38	33	33
Beverages	(ml)	140	159	142	159	151
Soft drinks including milk	(ml)	340	360	423	340	248
Alcoholic drinks	(ml)	681	558	579	665	680
Confectionery		22	18	20	18	18
Household Expenditure		*pence per person per week unless otherwise stated*				
Milk and cream		146.7	146.4	131.3	147.1	154.1
Cheese		47.8	65.0	60.0	58.3	68.1
Carcase meat		104.6	103.3	107.6	105.3	110.1
Other meat and meat products		345.2	373.2	343.7	395.5	386.7
Fish		83.3	108.7	116.4	85.7	101.4
Eggs		16.1	17.5	20.1	17.4	18.1
Fats and oils		35.8	37.4	33.1	34.1	39.3
Sugar and preserves		16.1	16.2	15.8	13.8	18.3
Potatoes		102.6	99.2	81.2	111.2	96.6
Vegetables		150.9	192.9	201.6	149.9	204.7
Fruit		137.9	183.6	193.9	139.8	197.0
Total Cereals		321.8	373.0	360.6	387.9	389.9
Beverages		39.2	40.7	31.6	35.5	48.1
Soft drinks		65.4	71.3	77.5	104.4	73.7
Alcoholic drinks		233.6	244.9	223.4	257.6	265.4
Confectionery		83.6	78.5	60.2	85.7	78.5
Total all food & drink excluding alcohol		1805.1	2031.5	1952.7	1996.6	2115.3
Total all food & drink		2038.7	2276.3	2176.1	2254.2	2380.7
Eating Out Expenditure		*pence per person per week unless otherwise stated*				
Total all food & drink excluding alcohol		590.1	695.8	959.5	775.3	629.6
Total all food & drink		962.7	972.0	1355.5	1127.2	936.2

(a) Converted to unconcentrated equivalent by applying a factor of 5 to concentrated and low calorie concentrated soft drinks

Table 6.6 Energy and nutrient intakes from all food and drink by region 2002-03

England & Regions		England	North East	North West	Yorkshire and The Humber	East Midlands	West Midlands	East	London	South East	South West
Number of households in sample		5400	318	747	560	438	558	638	605	920	616
Average age of HRP		52	51	51	52	51	51	51	49.6	51.1	55
Average number of adults per household		1.86	1.83	1.88	1.82	1.86	1.94	1.85	1.86	1.88	1.83
Average number of children per household		0.53	0.61	0.55	0.51	0.59	0.55	0.53	0.59	0.53	0.37
Average gross weekly household income (£)		561.74	465.17	490.84	472.8	538.49	488.63	581.29	771.73	644.65	510.95
Total Energy & Nutrient Intakes[a]										*intake per person per day*	
Energy	kcal	2310	2390	2720	2360	2320	2310	2260	2190	2310	2450
	MJ	9.7	10	11.4	9.9	9.8	9.7	9.5	9.2	9.7	10.3
Total Protein	g	77.7	79	94.1	80	78.2	76.6	76.7	74.3	77.9	82.2
Fat	g	93	98	112	96	94	93	91	87	95	100
Fatty acids:											
Saturates	g	36.3	38.8	42.5	37.4	36.8	35.8	36.0	32.3	37.0	39.7
Mono-unsaturates	g	33.8	35.6	42	34.8	33.8	34	33.1	31.6	34.2	35.9
Poly-unsaturates	g	16.7	16.9	19.7	16.8	16.4	17.0	15.8	17	16.9	17.3
Cholesterol	mg	260	270	300	271	256	253	258	250	259	280
Carbohydrate[b]	g	288	294	333	294	290	290	284	278	285	304
Total sugars	g	136	142	140	137	138	133	139	123	138	148
Non-milk extr sugars	g	92	101	96	94	94	91	94	82	93	98
Starch	g	151	152	193	157	151	156	145	155	147	156
Fibre[c]	g	14.5	13.8	16.5	14.6	14.6	14.3	14.8	14.1	14.7	15.8
Alcohol	g	11	13	13	11	11	11	10	9	11	12
Calcium	mg	990	1010	1100	1000	1030	1010	980	890	990	1080
Iron	mg	11.9	11.7	13.6	12.2	12.1	11.8	11.9	11.1	12.1	13
Zinc	mg	9.2	9.3	10.9	9.5	9.3	9.1	9.1	8.8	9.2	9.9
Magnesium	mg	283	285	332	286	287	278	281	267	289	306
Sodium[d]	g	3.02	3.22	3.56	3.08	3.08	2.99	3.01	2.63	3.09	3.2
Potassium	g	3.15	3.16	3.77	3.18	3.19	3.13	3.15	2.91	3.2	3.43
Thiamin	mg	1.63	1.61	1.84	1.67	1.64	1.63	1.62	1.51	1.65	1.76
Riboflavin	mg	1.97	1.98	2.14	2.02	2.01	1.95	1.95	1.74	1.99	2.2
Niacin Equivalent	mg	34	34.7	41.1	35.2	34.1	33.4	33.6	32.1	34.3	36
Vitamin B6	mg	2.4	2.5	2.8	2.5	2.4	2.4	2.4	2.2	2.4	2.6
Vitamin B12	µg	6.2	6.4	7	6.7	6.1	6.0	6.2	5.8	6.1	6.7
Folate	µg	290	279	302	294	288	288	294	272	297	323
Vitamin C	mg	75	66	78	72	71	70	80	78	80	80
Vitamin A:											
Retinol	µg	540	520	540	600	490	500	570	490	570	630
β-carotene	µg	1920	1860	2040	1890	1930	1870	2040	1810	1970	2200
Retinol equivalent	µg	870	840	890	920	820	820	920	800	900	1010
Vitamin D	µg	3.53	3.44	3.84	3.67	3.51	3.62	3.58	3.27	3.56	3.76
Vitamin E	mg	12.47	12.29	16.59	12.43	12.53	12.97	12.06	12.49	12.59	13.03
								as a percentage of total food & drink energy			
Fat	%	36.4	37.4	36.5	36.9	36.8	36.9	36.8	36.2	37.3	37.2
Fatty acids:											
Saturates	%	14.2	14.8	14.4	14.4	14.5	14.2	14.5	13.4	14.6	14.8
Mono-unsaturates	%	13.2	13.6	13.2	13.5	13.3	13.5	13.4	13.2	13.5	13.4
Poly-unsaturates	%	6.5	6.4	6.4	6.5	6.4	6.7	6.4	7.1	6.6	6.4
Carbohydrate	%	46.8	45.4	45.9	46.1	46.2	46.5	46.5	47.2	45.7	45.9

(a) Contributions from pharmaceutical sources are not recorded by the Survey
(b) Available carbohydrate, calculated as monosaccharide
(c) As non-starch polysaccharides
(d) Excludes sodium from table salt

Chapter 7: Demographic comparisons

This section contains comparisons based on the characteristics of the household or the Household Reference Person. A degree of caution in interpretation is required because the sampling errors at these levels can be high, especially where the sample size is small. The sample size is given at the top of each column as an indication of the reliability of the figures.

The consumption and expenditure tables contain data from both household food and drink and eating out. The energy and nutrient intake tables not only include the combined intakes from food brought into the home and eaten out but also the contributions from soft drinks, alcoholic drinks and confectionery.

For a more detailed breakdown of the data, please refer to the datasets which are published on the Defra website at:
http://statistics.defra.gov.uk/esg/publications/efs/default.asp

Income quintile

Table 7.1 shows average consumption and expenditure for both household and food and drink eaten out by income quintile, based on gross weekly household income. Table 7.2 shows the average daily energy and nutrient intake from all food and drink by income quintile. The first income quintile contains the lowest income households. The fifth or highest income quintile contains the households with the highest income. There are 5 quintiles in all, each representing twenty per cent of the population of households.

There is little evidence of a clear trend in nutrient intake with income. Total energy and fat intake is highest in income quintile 2 and lowest in income quintile 3. Income quintile 5 has the highest intakes of some vitamins and minerals including iron, folate and vitamin C, while income quintile 1 generally has the lowest intakes, although for calcium, vitamin B12, vitamin A and vitamin D the highest intakes were found in quintile 1. The percentage of energy derived from total fat, saturated and mono-unsaturated fatty acids, and carbohydrate is higher in the lower income groups. Intake of alcohol increases through each income group.

First income quintile households

For food and drink brought into the home, households in the first income quintile are the highest consumers of milk and cream, fish, eggs, fats and oils, sugar and preserves, cereals and beverages but consume the lowest amounts of carcase meat, soft drinks and alcohol. This probably reflects a tendency towards a basic diet and avoidance of expensive foodstuffs in the households with the highest average HRP age and lowest levels of income. Members of these households also have the lowest consumption and expenditure of food and drink eaten outside the home with only 21 per cent of the total food and drink expenditure being spent on eating out, compared to 40 per cent in fifth quintile households. First income quintile households spend 14 per cent less than the UK average on household food and drink but 55 per cent less on food eaten out. Households in the first income quintile have higher percentages of energy derived from fat, fatty acids and carbohydrate than those in the higher income groups. Intakes of most vitamins and minerals are lowest in these households although for calcium and vitamins A, B_{12} and D they are highest.

Second income quintile households

Home consumption of all meat and meat products, potatoes and confectionery is highest and consumption of cheese lowest, in second income quintile households. These households spend 7.1 per cent less on household food and drink and 37 per cent less on food and drink eaten out than the UK average. 25 per cent of the total food and drink expenditure is spent on eating out. Households in the second income quintile have the highest average energy intake and the highest intakes of fat and carbohydrate.

Third income quintile households

Households in the third income quintile have the lowest consumption of non-carcase meat and meat products, fish, vegetables (excluding potatoes) and fruit. They spend 7.2 per cent less than the UK average on household food and drink and 14 per cent less on eating out. However, spending on eating out represents 32 per cent of the total food and drink expenditure in these households which is nearly equivalent to the UK average of 33 per cent. Third income quintile households have the lowest energy and fat intakes but they do not have the lowest percentage of energy derived from fat.

Fourth income quintile households

Members of fourth income quintile households have the highest home consumption of soft drinks with over 3.6 per cent of expenditure on food and drink in the home being spent on this item. Household food and drink expenditure is 1.7 per cent higher and eating out expenditure 9.9 per cent higher than the average for all UK households.

Fifth income quintile households

Households in the fifth income quintile have the highest home consumption of cheese, vegetables (excluding potatoes), fruit and alcoholic drinks and the lowest consumption of milk and cream, fats, sugar, potatoes, cereals, beverages and confectionery. These households also have the highest consumption and expenditure of food and drink eaten outside the home with 40 per cent of the total food and drink expenditure being spent on eating out, compared to the UK average of 33 per cent. Their household food and drink expenditure is 16 per cent above the UK average. In contrast, their expenditure on food and drink eaten out is 53 per cent higher. Fifth income quintile households have the highest intakes of some vitamins and minerals including iron, folate and vitamin C and also the highest fibre and alcohol intakes. In contrast, the percentage of energy derived from fat, fatty acids and carbohydrate is lowest in fifth income quintile households.

Table 7.1 Consumption and expenditure of selected foods by income quintile 2002-03

Income Quintiles		Quintile 1	Quintile 2	Quintile 3	Quintile 4	Quintile 5
Number of households in sample		1424	1447	1416	1359	1281
Average age of HRP		60	57	49	46	45
Average number of adults per household		1.25	1.67	1.88	2.16	2.42
Average number of children per household		0.28	0.41	0.61	0.69	0.71
Lower boundary (gross weekly household income (£))		0	187.86	341.44	541.21	820.95
Household Consumption		*grams per person per week unless otherwise stated*				
Milk and cream	(ml)	2261	2152	2011	1936	1785
Cheese		100	98	107	114	128
Carcase meat		212	248	220	244	221
Other meat and meat products		823	825	786	809	810
Fish		168	166	140	144	161
Eggs	(no.)	2.2	1.9	1.6	1.5	1.5
Fats and oils		230	221	189	178	159
Sugar and preserves		207	193	150	123	102
Potatoes		944	969	883	879	738
Vegetables		1090	1127	1027	1101	1140
Fruit		1128	1147	1095	1224	1356
Total Cereals		1756	1736	1669	1638	1596
Beverages		74	67	59	53	49
Soft drinks [a]	(ml)	1568	1648	1810	1924	1723
Alcoholic drinks	(ml)	484	623	664	804	891
Confectionery		123	138	129	127	120
Eating Out Consumption		*grams per person per week unless otherwise stated*				
Ethnic meals		8	13	17	25	38
Meat and meat products		47	73	93	106	124
Fish and fish products		7	12	13	15	19
Cheese and egg dishes and pizza		12	16	24	30	36
Potatoes		45	68	88	95	106
Vegetables		19	26	35	35	46
Sandwiches		29	49	66	93	126
Ice creams, desserts and cakes		17	25	31	36	40
Beverages	(ml)	88	124	146	163	177
Soft drinks including milk	(ml)	165	271	356	418	525
Alcoholic drinks	(ml)	404	526	660	792	915
Confectionery		12	23	24	24	24
Household Expenditure		*pence per person per week unless otherwise stated*				
Milk and cream		154.4	146.0	144.2	146.2	148.0
Cheese		47.2	47.4	53.1	58.7	73.4
Carcase meat		92.5	108.0	102.4	110.4	111.2
Other meat and meat products		316.4	331.2	340.7	370.4	421.9
Fish		90.1	92.6	79.6	88.1	109.0
Eggs		20.8	17.7	15.9	15.2	18.2
Fats and oils		41.5	40.7	35.5	33.8	35.5
Sugar and preserves		20.9	18.7	15.7	14.5	13.9
Potatoes		92.1	99.2	97.8	103.1	98.0
Vegetables		140.0	147.8	147.9	174.5	213.9
Fruit		136.5	143.3	142.9	158.5	194.7
Total Cereals		320.1	345.3	345.9	372.7	413.3
Beverages		46.6	47.6	41.4	40.8	38.3
Soft drinks		57.7	67.7	72.4	81.3	80.6
Alcoholic drinks		153.8	194.3	216.7	265.5	341.4
Confectionery		67.4	79.4	75.2	77.6	79.6
Total all food & drink excluding alcohol		1736.1	1841.3	1815.9	1963.0	2190.5
Total all food & drink		1889.9	2035.6	2032.6	2228.5	2531.8
Eating Out Expenditure		*pence per person per week unless otherwise stated*				
Total all food & drink excluding alcohol		324.4	454.2	623.6	776.8	1117.5
Total all food & drink		497.4	689.8	944.1	1202.1	1671.2

(a) Converted to unconcentrated equivalent by applying a factor of 5 to concentrated and low calorie concentrated soft drinks

Table 7.2 Energy & nutrient intakes from all food & drink by income quintile 2002-03

Income Quintiles		Quintile 1	Quintile 2	Quintile 3	Quintile 4	Quintile 5
Number of households in sample		1424	1447	1416	1359	1281
Average age of HRP		60	57	49	46	45
Average number of adults per household		1.25	1.67	1.88	2.16	2.42
Average number of children per household		0.28	0.41	0.61	0.69	0.71
Lower boundary (gross weekly household income (£))			187.86	341.44	541.21	820.95
Total Energy & Nutrient Intakes[a]					*intakes per person per day*	
Energy	kcal	2250	2330	2240	2280	2260
	MJ	9.4	9.8	9.4	9.6	9.5
Total Protein	g	75.6	77.4	74.8	77.5	78.1
Fat	g	93	96	91	93	92
Fatty acids:						
Saturates	g	36.7	38.1	35.7	36.0	35.9
Mono-unsaturates	g	33.7	34.8	33.2	33.8	33.3
Poly-unsaturates	g	16.5	16.9	16.2	16.7	16.2
Cholesterol	mg	270	269	249	254	261
Carbohydrate[b]	g	281	291	280	280	274
Total sugars	g	137	143	134	135	130
Non-milk extr sugars	g	93	99	93	92	87
Starch	g	144	147	145	145	144
Fibre[c]	g	13.4	14.1	13.6	14.1	14.3
Alcohol	g	7	9	10	12	14
Calcium	mg	1020	1010	980	990	970
Iron	mg	11.2	11.7	11.4	11.9	12.1
Zinc	mg	9.0	9.2	9.0	9.2	9.2
Magnesium	mg	265	275	269	280	284
Sodium[d]	g	2.92	3.03	2.98	3.08	3.07
Potassium	g	2.92	3.03	2.93	3.05	3.06
Thiamin	mg	1.50	1.57	1.55	1.61	1.61
Riboflavin	mg	1.99	2.02	1.92	1.96	1.93
Niacin Equivalent	mg	31.7	33.1	32.6	34.4	34.8
Vitamin B6	mg	2.1	2.2	2.2	2.3	2.3
Vitamin B12	µg	6.6	6.4	6.0	6.2	6.1
Folate	µg	264	275	268	277	284
Vitamin C	mg	63	66	66	72	77
Vitamin A:						
Retinol	µg	580	560	510	510	540
β-carotene	µg	1810	1910	1770	1910	2000
Retinol equivalent	µg	890	880	820	830	880
Vitamin D	µg	3.76	3.64	3.39	3.49	3.40
Vitamin E	mg	12.21	12.62	12.09	12.57	12.12
				as a percentage of total food & drink energy		
Fat	%	37.4	37.3	36.7	36.7	36.5
Fatty acids:						
Saturates	%	14.7	14.7	14.3	14.2	14.3
Mono-unsaturates	%	13.5	13.5	13.3	13.3	13.2
Poly-unsaturates	%	6.6	6.5	6.5	6.6	6.4
Carbohydrate	%	46.9	46.8	46.8	46.0	45.3

(a) Contributions from pharmaceutical sources are not recorded by the Survey
(b) Available carbohydrate, calculated as monosaccharide
(c) As non-starch polysaccharides
(d) Excludes sodium from table salt

Household composition

The size and composition of a household, together with the age of the HRP and average gross weekly household income, have a significant effect on food consumption, expenditure and energy and nutrient intakes. Table 7.3 shows average consumption and expenditure for both household and food and drink eaten out by household composition. Table 7.4 shows the average daily energy and nutrient intake from all food and drink by household composition.

Adult only households

The trend in previous years for household food and drink consumption and expenditure to be highest in households with one, two or three adults and no children continues. On average, adult only households spend 11 per cent more than the UK average on food and drink eaten at home and 33 per cent more on eating out. Expenditure on food eaten at home remains highest in one adult households but when alcohol is included, two adult households have the highest household expenditure. Households with 4 or more adults and no children have the highest spend on eating out which accounts for 47 per cent of the household's total food and drink expenditure and is 67 per cent higher than the UK average. As expected, households that contain only adults have the highest average daily intake of energy per person and, as a consequence, higher intakes of all nutrients.

Households with children

Households with children continue to have the lowest levels of consumption in all foods, with the exception of soft drinks which is highest in single parent households. On average, households with children spend 25 per cent less (22 per cent less in 2001-02) than the UK average on food and drink eaten at home and 31 per cent less on eating out. For most food items the lowest levels of consumption and expenditure are in households with 3 or more adults and 3 or more children, where household expenditure is 45 per cent less and eating out expenditure 51 per cent less than the UK average. Households with 3 or more children have the lowest energy intake per person which reflects the lower energy requirements of children. In addition, these households have the lowest intakes of almost all nutrients.

Table 7.3 Consumption & expenditure of selected foods by household composition 2002-03

			Households with given number of adults and children

Household composition	Adults		1	1	2	2	2	2	2	3 or more		4 or more
	Children		0	1 or more	0	1	2	3	4 or more	0	1 or 2	3 or more	0

Number of households in sample		1853	497	2345	536	696	215	75	358	206	27	119
Average age of HRP		59	35	56	40	39	38	40	54	47	43	49
Average gross weekly household income (£)		275.80	281.33	555.80	737.70	758.81	715.07	1419.45	791.37	850.30	683.01	1049.25

Household consumption — *grams per person per week unless otherwise stated*

Milk and cream	(ml)	2501	1700	2210	2015	1804	1630	1706	1933	1687	1268	1674
Cheese		120	84	137	111	99	73	69	119	96	87	109
Carcase meat		215	122	301	216	165	147	150	312	246	115	245
Other meat and meat products		945	698	895	794	696	612	627	948	769	504	739
Fish		217	99	206	126	105	116	68	164	128	64	125
Eggs	(no.)	2.2	1.2	2.0	1.5	1.1	1.1	1.1	2.0	1.4	1.0	1.8
Fats and oils		242	130	239	155	132	136	135	204	171	224	202
Sugar and preserves		220	118	185	92	94	85	111	170	121	160	123
Potatoes		873	739	1023	827	741	735	650	949	845	692	787
Vegetables		1283	705	1411	1024	842	690	678	1315	960	610	995
Fruit		1617	696	1583	1117	942	774	679	1261	870	522	1094
Total Cereals		1938	1412	1819	1597	1490	1316	1512	1778	1579	1371	1680
Beverages		88	38	79	47	35	31	32	63	43	33	54
Soft drinks [a]	(ml)	1380	2124	1462	1963	2052	2008	2057	1816	1878	1542	1777
Alcoholic drinks	(ml)	803	389	908	783	650	468	302	877	491	284	799
Confectionery		136	121	136	127	134	128	116	112	115	104	82

Eating out consumption — *grams per person per week unless otherwise stated*

Ethnic meals		27	10	23	21	18	16	19	39	19	15	34
Meat and meat products		83	79	86	104	95	94	85	107	128	97	125
Fish and fish products		17	7	19	11	10	8	11	17	14	7	12
Cheese and egg dishes and pizza		24	21	20	25	30	26	27	29	38	31	36
Potatoes		78	77	82	85	90	90	98	87	96	94	93
Vegetables		43	18	44	31	26	20	13	44	29	23	39
Sandwiches		79	53	82	89	73	58	46	103	92	28	129
Ice creams, desserts and cakes		26	28	33	28	36	33	46	33	28	32	24
Beverages	(ml)	192	56	190	139	122	67	41	183	124	78	151
Soft drinks including milk	(ml)	219	389	278	427	431	440	485	398	586	419	601
Alcoholic drinks	(ml)	889	171	789	590	375	288	147	1419	765	187	1465
Confectionery		9	41	10	23	32	39	57	14	33	29	26

Household expenditure — *pence per person per week unless otherwise stated*

Milk and cream	187.1	115.2	166.1	154.5	138.5	113.7	108.6	142.3	118.3	83.3	122.8
Cheese	63.6	40.1	73.6	58.3	51.1	34.7	30.4	61.3	48.5	41.4	52.2
Carcase meat	111.3	48.8	145.8	95.0	74.2	59.6	57.4	145.8	100.3	40.9	107.9
Other meat and meat products	430.7	267.1	410.7	368.0	323.9	258.2	239.9	426.9	339.3	196.5	347.7
Fish	130.5	48.9	130.7	76.4	64.1	50.2	32.0	102.1	73.1	29.8	76.6
Eggs	24.6	10.9	21.8	16.7	11.3	9.5	8.6	20.4	14.3	9.2	16.8
Fats and oils	52.7	21.3	49.9	30.0	23.6	22.5	18.8	39.2	26.2	25.2	39.9
Sugar and preserves	26.4	10.4	21.5	10.9	10.3	7.9	11.6	18.3	11.1	13.1	12.6
Potatoes	94.7	101.2	100.5	103.5	96.9	90.4	94.6	101.8	105.0	69.0	93.0
Vegetables	211.9	97.5	221.1	170.5	135.1	95.5	82.4	197.3	136.5	73.8	145.3
Fruit	223.6	82.4	217.4	149.1	122.8	91.9	70.4	161.3	104.0	57.7	136.1
Total Cereals	413.5	302.1	398.0	384.4	347.1	282.1	293.0	387.8	324.9	277.5	368.9
Beverages	63.5	24.5	58.8	35.4	27.4	20.3	19.6	45.5	29.1	23.1	34.4
Soft drinks	61.5	81.1	65.2	84.0	84.1	74.5	70.3	76.2	86.1	59.2	76.9
Alcoholic drinks	311.9	118.6	342.6	238.6	202.8	141.1	77.4	293.7	141.7	66.1	230.7
Confectionery	82.7	72.5	81.6	80.7	82.2	74.7	65.7	67.6	67.9	54.4	50.7
Total all food & drink excluding alcohol	2305.7	1406.7	2298.6	1947.4	1695.6	1370.1	1277.0	2115.5	1695.5	1134.1	1787.3
Total all food & drink	2617.6	1525.3	2641.1	2185.9	1898.4	1511.2	1354.3	2409.1	1837.2	1200.2	2018.0

Eating out consumption — *pence per person per week unless otherwise stated*

Total all food & drink excluding alcohol	738.2	439.6	831.9	734.5	636.9	521.8	468.3	873.6	710.3	412.5	910.6
Total all food & drink	1177.2	542.3	1263.5	1051.9	837.6	659.7	546.2	1561.8	1105.4	531.8	1824.5

(a) Converted to unconcentrated equivalent by applying a factor of 5 to concentrated and low calorie concentrated soft drinks

Table 7.4 Energy & nutrient intakes from all food & drink by household composition 2002-03

		\multicolumn{10}{c}{Households with given number of adults and children}
Household composition	Adults	1	1	2	2	2	2	2	3 or more		4 or more
	Children	0	1 or more	0	1	2	3	4 or more	0	1 or 2	3 or more	0
Number of households in sample		1853	497	2345	536	696	215	75	358	206	27	119
Average age of HRP		59	35	56	40	39	38	40	54	47	43	49
Average gross weekly household income (£)		275.8	281.3	555.8	737.7	758.8	715.1	1419.5	791.4	850.3	683.0	1049.3
Total energy & nutrient intakes [a]											*intakes per person per day*	
Energy	kcal	2600	1900	2570	2210	2020	1840	1950	2510	2210	1840	2290
	MJ	10.9	8.0	10.8	9.3	8.5	7.7	8.2	10.5	9.3	7.7	9.6
Total Protein	g	88.9	60.7	88.8	75.0	66.3	58.8	60.5	87.0	74.1	51.6	76.2
Fat	g	105.0	77.0	105.0	89.0	81.0	75.0	77.0	100.0	89.0	80.0	89.0
Fatty acids:												
Saturates	g	41.9	30.3	41.0	35.4	31.9	29.4	30.3	38.6	33.7	27.5	33.9
Mono-unsaturates	g	37.5	28.0	37.8	32.3	29.4	27.3	28.4	36.5	32.6	29.3	32.5
Poly-unsaturates	g	18.2	13.5	18.5	15.5	14.2	13.3	13.5	18.0	16.5	18.1	16.8
Cholesterol	mg	314	196	303	246	210	187	186	296	240	169	253
Carbohydrate [b]	g	322	248	313	275	260	237	263	306	282	237	287
Total sugars	g	156	119	149	129	124	113	119	142	126	112	127
Non-milk extr sugars	g	102	87	98	87	87	81	87	96	89	85	88
Starch	g	166	129	164	146	136	123	143	164	156	125	160
Fibre [c]	g	16.7	10.7	16.8	13.6	12.3	11.0	11.4	15.6	13.3	9.7	13.7
Alcohol	g	13.0	4.0	14.0	10.0	8.0	6.0	3.0	16.0	9.0	3.0	15.0
Calcium	mg	1170	830	1110	970	890	790	830	1050	920	690	940
Iron	mg	13.7	9.2	13.6	11.5	10.5	9.3	9.8	12.7	11.1	8.3	11.3
Zinc	mg	10.6	7.2	10.6	9.0	7.9	7.1	7.2	10.2	8.9	6.4	9.0
Magnesium	mg	332	211	328	271	241	214	212	309	258	186	276
Sodium [d]	g	3.48	2.54	3.38	2.98	2.73	2.37	2.37	3.29	2.80	2.10	2.91
Potassium	g	3.64	2.40	3.67	3.02	2.66	2.37	2.36	3.44	2.87	2.06	3.00
Thiamin	mg	1.83	1.28	1.84	1.59	1.45	1.29	1.35	1.76	1.55	1.16	1.56
Riboflavin	mg	2.35	1.54	2.26	1.89	1.71	1.54	1.58	2.09	1.77	1.30	1.85
Niacin Equivalent	mg	38.1	26.2	38.6	32.9	29.3	26.0	26.3	38.8	32.3	22.2	33.8
Vitamin B6	mg	2.7	1.9	2.8	2.3	2.1	1.9	1.9	2.7	2.3	1.7	2.4
Vitamin B12	µg	7.6	4.8	7.3	5.8	5.2	4.8	4.7	6.7	5.7	3.9	5.6
Folate	µg	338	206	341	271	242	216	215	322	262	188	286
Vitamin C	mg	86	54	88	74	63	55	52	78	62	44	71
Vitamin A:												
Retinol	µg	700	340	700	460	390	330	340	570	470	380	450
β-carotene	µg	2150	1340	2300	1790	1590	1280	1260	2280	1550	1110	1930
Retinol equivalent	µg	1070	570	1090	760	660	550	550	960	730	570	780
Vitamin D	µg	4.41	2.60	4.10	3.44	2.90	2.73	2.66	3.74	2.97	2.31	3.20
Vitamin E	mg	13.68	10.18	13.69	11.78	10.79	10.27	10.48	13.03	12.10	13.36	12.55
											as a percentage of total food & drink energy	
Fat	%	36.7	36.8	37.2	37.0	36.4	37.3	35.9	36.5	36.3	39.2	35.5
Fatty acids:												
Saturates	%	14.7	14.5	14.5	14.7	14.4	14.6	14.1	14.0	13.8	13.5	13.5
Mono-unsaturates	%	13.1	13.4	13.5	13.4	13.2	13.6	13.2	13.3	13.3	14.3	13.0
Poly-unsaturates	%	6.4	6.4	6.6	6.4	6.4	6.6	6.2	6.6	6.7	8.9	6.6
Carbohydrate	%	45.9	48.6	45.0	46.3	47.7	47.8	50.1	45.1	47.2	48.1	46.3

(a) Contributions from pharmaceutical sources are not recorded by the Survey
(b) Available carbohydrate, calculated as monosaccharide
(c) As non-starch polysaccharides
(d) Excludes sodium from table salt

Age group of household reference person

From 2001-02 the concept of Household Reference Person (HRP) was adopted on all government-sponsored surveys replacing the concept of head of household. The HRP is the person who:

- owns the household accommodation or
- is legally responsible for the rent of the accommodation or
- has the household accommodation as an emolument or perquisite or
- has the household accommodation by virtue of some relationship to the owner who is not a member of the household.

If more than one person meet these criteria the HRP will be the one with the higher income. If the incomes are the same then the eldest is chosen.

The age of the HRP is often related to the composition of the household and, to a lesser extent, its income group and level of eating out. In particular it is necessary to consider the average number of children per household before interpreting the results. For example, there are practically no children in households where the HRP is aged between 65 and 74, leading to higher average energy intakes per person than in households with children. The survey results by the HRP age group should therefore be interpreted with caution. Table 7.5 shows average consumption and expenditure for both household and food and drink eaten out by HRP age group. Table 7.6 shows the average daily energy and nutrient intake from all food and drink by HRP age group.

Table 7.6 shows that average intakes of energy and all nutrients are lowest in the "under 30" HRP age group partly due to the higher number of children in these households. Similarly, average intakes of energy and most nutrients are highest in the "65 and under 75" HRP age group, where the number of children in these households would be lower.

Household and eating out

As shown previously, household consumption of most food items rises steadily with the age of the HRP to a peak in the "65 and under 75" age group. The exceptions are sugar and beverages which continue to rise with age, soft drinks which peak with the "40 and under 50" age group and cheese together with non-carcase meat which peak at age 50 and under 65. The consumption of food and drink items eaten out shows more variation across the age groups but overall consumption of most food and drink items is lowest in the "75 and over" age group.

Household reference person aged less than thirty

Household consumption of all foods except fish, and both soft and alcoholic drinks, is lowest in households where the HRP is aged less than 30. For alcoholic drinks from both home supplies and eating out, members of these households consume the highest amounts. The per capita spend in these households is £17.59 on food and drink consumed at home which is 20 per cent less than the UK average for all households. They have the highest spend on food and drink eaten out at £14.71, which represents 46 per cent of their total expenditure on all food and drink, and is 35 per cent above the UK average. Intakes of energy and all nutrients are lowest in the "under 30" age group.

Household reference person aged between thirty and under forty

Households where the HRP is aged 30 and under 40 have the lowest home consumption of fish and alcoholic drinks. Their expenditure on household food and drink (£18.88) is 14 per cent lower than the UK average. The percentage of energy derived from carbohydrate is highest in households within this group.

Household reference person aged between forty and under fifty

The highest consumption of soft drinks is in households where the HRP is aged 40 and under 50 and these households also have a high proportion of children. Of food and drink eaten out, these households are the largest consumers of cheese and egg dishes and pizza, chips, cakes and ice creams and confectionery, which might indicate a pattern of eating out driven by the preferences of children.

Household reference person aged between fifty and under sixty-five

Consumption and expenditure of alcoholic drinks brought into the home is highest in households where the HRP is aged 50 and under 65. These households have the highest eating out consumption of fish, vegetables and beverages. Also, they have the highest combined food and drink expenditure (£38.46) of which 32 per cent (£12.50) is spent on eating out which is 14 per cent more than the UK average. The per capita household expenditure at £25.96 is 18 per cent higher than the UK average.

Household reference person aged between sixty-five and under seventy-five

Home consumption of most food items, apart from cheese, non-carcase meat, sugar, beverages and soft and alcoholic drinks, is highest in households where the HRP is aged 65 and under 75. Members of households in this HRP age group have the highest expenditure on food and drink brought into the home (£26.07) which is 24 per cent more than the average for all UK households. Expenditure on eating out (£8.40) is 24 per cent of the total spend on food and drink. In addition, energy intakes and the intakes of most nutrients are highest in this age group.

Household reference person aged seventy-five and over

Members of households in the "aged 75 and over" group are the highest consumers of sugar and beverages and have the lowest consumption of soft and alcoholic drinks. Their expenditure on food and drink consumed at home (£23.32) is 6 per cent more than the UK average for all households whereas their expenditure on food and drink eaten out (£5.39) is 49 per cent below the UK average and represents only 19 per cent of their total expenditure on all food and drink. The percentage of energy derived from fat and saturated fat is highest in households within this group.

Table 7.5 Consumption & expenditure of selected foods by age of household reference person 2002-03

Age group of household reference person		under 30	30 and under 40	40 and under 50	50 and under 65	65 and under 75	75 and over
Number of households in sample		680	1409	1343	1682	1006	807
Average number of adults per household		1.72	1.81	2.14	2.03	1.69	1.45
Average number of children per household		0.68	1.23	0.94	0.14	0.02	0
Average gross weekly household income (£)		480.93	646.41	739.45	580.92	326.82	251.41

Household consumption					*grams per person per week unless otherwise stated*		
Milk and cream	(ml)	1498	1759	1852	2200	2546	2530
Cheese		92	100	104	137	127	102
Carcase meat		132	160	203	318	348	259
Other meat and meat products		649	692	818	962	917	776
Fish		116	109	134	191	228	216
Eggs	(no.)	1.3	1.3	1.4	2.1	2.3	2.1
Fats and oils		119	139	163	235	291	271
Sugar and preserves		76	96	115	184	251	253
Potatoes		641	704	847	1055	1123	868
Vegetables		781	898	967	1406	1477	1193
Fruit		812	962	1011	1521	1699	1590
Total Cereals		1363	1517	1601	1861	1991	1758
Beverages		32	37	46	77	94	97
Soft drinks [a]	(ml)	1975	1854	1979	1688	1467	971
Alcoholic drinks	(ml)	744	658	750	867	679	470
Confectionery		93	113	137	133	148	144

Eating out consumption					*grams per person per week unless otherwise stated*		
Ethnic meals		33	22	25	26	11	6
Meat and meat products		124	94	113	94	62	41
Fish and fish products		10	12	13	18	16	15
Cheese and egg dishes and pizza		33	26	33	26	13	7
Potatoes		96	88	97	82	68	55
Vegetables		37	28	33	41	37	32
Sandwiches		121	83	94	80	39	21
Ice creams, desserts and cakes		26	34	34	34	28	23
Beverages	(ml)	106	121	148	195	159	118
Soft drinks including milk	(ml)	516	423	502	325	152	59
Alcoholic drinks	(ml)	1028	523	702	901	637	310
Confectionery		25	30	33	15	5	2

Household expenditure				*pence per person per week unless otherwise stated*			
Milk and cream		106.8	132.2	135.2	161.8	189.9	193.4
Cheese		45.0	52.0	53.8	71.1	69.3	53.8
Carcase meat		52.3	67.2	93.0	153.4	162.6	135.8
Other meat and meat products		316.7	322.0	369.3	421.3	387.3	345.2
Fish		61.7	64.2	77.9	119.2	143.0	133.5
Eggs		12.3	13.3	14.0	22.1	24.2	23.5
Fats and oils		20.1	24.8	29.5	47.2	63.2	56.8
Sugar and preserves		7.3	10.1	12.4	20.9	28.9	29.0
Potatoes		93.0	95.4	103.2	106.7	98.3	77.6
Vegetables		126.9	152.7	154.0	212.4	201.2	171.2
Fruit		95.8	122.3	133.0	206.7	230.8	217.1
Total Cereals		342.2	343.7	367.9	391.7	387.6	364.3
Beverages		23.8	27.2	34.5	57.1	66.3	65.6
Soft drinks		78.1	77.1	84.0	73.4	62.2	41.5
Alcoholic drinks		208.5	208.6	238.3	319.8	265.9	229.9
Confectionery		56.8	68.2	84.5	78.8	88.9	84.1
Total all food & drink excluding alcohol		1539.2	1682.8	1859.4	2275.2	2329.7	2099.7
Total all food & drink		1747.8	1891.4	2097.7	2595.1	2595.7	2329.6

Eating out expenditure				*pence per person per week unless otherwise stated*			
Total all food & drink excluding alcohol		858.7	692.3	781.8	797.2	557.2	400.3
Total all food & drink		1471.3	995.0	1153.8	1249.7	840.0	538.5

(a) Converted to unconcentrated equivalent by applying a factor of 5 to concentrated and low calorie concentrated soft drinks

Table 7.6 Energy & nutrient intake from all food & drink by age of household reference person 2002-03

Age group of household reference person		under 30	30 and under 40	40 and under 50	50 and under 65	65 and under 75	75 and over
Number of households in sample		680	1409	1343	1682	1006	807
Average number of adults per household		1.72	1.81	2.14	2.03	1.69	1.45
Average number of children per household		0.68	1.23	0.94	0.14	0.02	0
Average gross weekly household income (£)		480.93	646.41	739.45	580.92	326.82	251.41
Total energy & nutrient intakes[a]						*intakes per person per day*	
Energy	kcal	1880	2000	2220	2590	2690	2360
	MJ	7.9	8.4	9.3	10.9	11.3	9.9
Total Protein	g	62.6	66.4	74.3	90.4	91.7	78.4
Fat	g	74.0	80.7	90.6	10.8	112.5	99.5
Fatty acids:							
Saturates	g	28.2	31.3	35.2	41.6	45.3	40.7
Mono-unsaturates	g	26.9	29.3	33.0	38.8	40.5	35.5
Poly-unsaturates	g	13.8	14.6	16.2	18.9	19.0	16.4
Cholesterol	mg	199	213	244	314	329	291
Carbohydrate[b]	g	235	254	274	312	328	291
Total sugars	g	109	118	131	151	165	154
Non-milk extr sugars	g	78	82	92	101	109	101
Starch	g	126	136	143	161	162	137
Fibre[c]	g	11.0	12.3	13.1	16.3	17.0	14.8
Alcohol	g	12	9	11	14	12	8
Calcium	mg	810	880	960	1120	1180	1060
Iron	mg	9.5	10.5	11.3	13.5	13.8	12.2
Zinc	mg	7.4	7.9	8.8	10.7	11.0	9.5
Magnesium	mg	225	240	265	323	330	286
Sodium[d]	g	2.65	2.71	2.99	3.44	3.42	2.94
Potassium	g	2.42	2.60	2.87	3.53	3.65	3.16
Thiamin	mg	1.30	1.42	1.53	1.80	1.85	1.58
Riboflavin	mg	1.52	1.69	1.86	2.26	2.41	2.22
Niacin Equivalent	mg	28.1	29.2	32.8	39.5	39.0	32.4
Vitamin B6	mg	1.9	2.0	2.2	2.6	2.6	2.2
Vitamin B12	µg	4.9	5.1	5.8	7.3	8.0	7.2
Folate	µg	220	236	259	325	338	296
Vitamin C	mg	60	62	64	82	85	74
Vitamin A:							
Retinol	µg	360	390	460	670	790	730
β-carotene	µg	1380	1550	1760	2330	2460	2100
Retinol equivalent	µg	590	660	760	1060	1220	1090
Vitamin D	µg	2.80	2.98	3.17	4.13	4.51	4.10
Vitamin E	mg	10.59	11.11	12.08	13.94	13.98	12.30
					as a percentage of total food and drink energy		
Fat	%	35.5	36.2	36.8	37.1	37.7	37.9
Fatty acids:							
Saturates	%	13.5	14.0	14.3	14.5	15.2	15.5
Mono-unsaturates	%	12.9	13.2	13.4	13.5	13.5	13.5
Poly-unsaturates	%	6.6	6.5	6.6	6.6	6.4	6.3
Carbohydrate	%	46.8	47.5	46.4	45.2	45.7	46.3

(a) Contributions from pharmaceutical sources are not recorded by the Survey
(b) Available carbohydrate, calculated as monosaccharide
(c) As non-starch polysaccharides
(d) Excludes sodium from table salt

Age at which household reference person ceased full-time education

The age at which the HRP ceased full-time education is related to the age of the HRP, the composition of the household, the level of eating out and, given that graduates earn more than non-graduates, the household income. It should be noted that in the aged 14 and under group there are fewer adults and children and the average age of the HRP is much older. These factors, and as they apply to each particular age group, should be taken into account when interpreting the results. Table 7.7 shows average consumption and expenditure for both household and food and drink eaten out by HRP education age group. Table 7.8 shows the average daily energy and nutrient intake from all food and drink by HRP education age group.

Household

Home consumption of milk and cream, fats, sugars, cereals, beverages and confectionery is highest, and consumption of soft and alcoholic drinks lowest, in households where the HRP ceased full-time education aged 14 and under. The highest consumption of all meat and meat products and potatoes is in households in the "aged 15" group. Households in the "aged 16" group have the highest consumption of soft drinks and the lowest consumption of fish, fats, vegetables, fruit and cereals. Consumption of cheese, fish, vegetables, fruit and alcoholic drinks is highest, and of all meat, sugars, potatoes, beverages and confectionery lowest, in households where the HRP ceased full-time education aged 22 or more.

Eating out

There are marked differences in the patterns of eating out with people in households where the HRP ceased full-time education "aged 14 and under" group having the lowest consumption and expenditure, which accounts for only 21 per cent of their total food and drink expenditure. Higher eating out consumption levels are recorded in households where the HRP ceased full-time education aged 19 and under 22 and aged 22 and over, where 36 per cent of the total food and drink expenditure is spent on eating out.

Intakes

As in 2001-02, energy and the intakes of most nutrients are lowest in households where the HRP ceased full-time education aged 16. This year energy and most nutrient intakes are highest in households where the HRP ceased full-time education aged 15.

Table 7.7 Consumption & expenditure of selected foods by age at which household reference person ceased full-time education 2002-03

Age at which household reference person ceased full time education	Aged 14 & under	Aged 15	Aged 16	Aged 17 & under 19	Aged 19 & under 22	Aged 22 & over
Number of households in sample	971	1357	2148	1140	659	622
Average age of HRP	73	57	45	46	45	43
Average number of adults per household	1.6	1.89	1.89	1.88	1.9	1.95
Average number of children per household	0.07	0.29	0.81	0.64	0.63	0.54
Average gross weekly household income (£)	243.87	400.58	511.09	606.22	750.77	1070.97

Household consumption — *grams per person per week unless otherwise stated*

Milk and cream	(ml)	2341	2115	1930	1885	1862	2001
Cheese		96	118	102	118	120	132
Carcase meat		286	294	209	218	212	172
Other meat and meat products		839	944	826	775	715	647
Fish		188	159	131	157	153	196
Eggs	(no.)	2.1	1.9	1.5	1.5	1.6	1.6
Fats and oils		274	233	160	177	176	165
Sugar and preserves		265	186	123	122	118	110
Potatoes		1019	1118	873	790	664	607
Vegetables		1194	1195	949	1073	1208	1301
Fruit		1306	1111	957	1289	1529	1682
Total Cereals		1871	1798	1588	1629	1640	1591
Beverages		92	71	51	52	50	49
Soft drinks[a]	(ml)	1225	1846	1990	1788	1609	1388
Alcoholic drinks	(ml)	497	762	685	750	800	903
Confectionery		147	134	132	126	123	89

Eating out consumption — *grams per person per week unless otherwise stated*

Ethnic meals		6	18	18	27	37	36
Meat and meat products		52	90	101	105	106	90
Fish and fish products		13	13	12	15	18	18
Cheese and egg dishes and pizza		12	22	26	30	27	33
Potatoes		58	75	92	93	94	86
Vegetables		28	34	30	40	44	39
Sandwiches		30	63	78	92	107	115
Ice creams, desserts and cakes		22	26	30	37	41	40
Beverages	(ml)	122	163	141	155	144	149
Soft drinks including milk	(ml)	141	313	426	395	437	418
Alcoholic drinks	(ml)	449	820	679	770	664	648
Confectionery		8	20	28	22	22	19

Household expenditure — *pence per person per week unless otherwise stated*

Milk and cream	166.8	147.4	138.7	147.7	147.2	160.7
Cheese	49.0	55.2	50.5	62.7	67.8	80.3
Carcase meat	134.9	132.6	89.7	105.2	107.9	91.3
Other meat and meat products	336.8	387.7	366.0	375.4	353.5	339.9
Fish	113.7	92.8	75.3	93.7	103.7	123.9
Eggs	20.5	18.8	14.8	16.6	18.7	19.5
Fats and oils	53.2	42.9	29.4	34.8	39.8	36.6
Sugar and preserves	26.2	17.9	12.4	15.3	16.7	17.5
Potatoes	90.9	110.6	107.0	93.2	88.5	77.2
Vegetables	152.0	157.8	140.0	183.1	214.9	250.2
Fruit	171.6	141.3	122.1	172.5	210.5	237.8
Total Cereals	356.7	355.8	352.2	381.3	392.2	394.9
Beverages	58.8	50.3	36.7	39.3	40.0	39.4
Soft drinks	51.3	73.3	80.9	75.1	74.1	70.0
Alcoholic drinks	189.2	229.7	210.6	266.1	322.7	370.0
Confectionery	82.2	76.8	78.8	76.2	80.3	63.1
Total all food & drink excluding alcohol	1970.6	1968.1	1801.9	1999.2	2084.2	2148.5
Total all food & drink	2159.8	2197.8	2012.5	2265.3	2406.9	2518.4

Eating out expenditure — *pence per person per week unless otherwise stated*

Total all food & drink excluding alcohol	387.5	568.6	657.0	849.7	999.6	1011.2
Total all food & drink	577.9	941.7	999.7	1288.8	1403.2	1447.0

(a) Converted to unconcentrated equivalent by applying a factor of 5 to concentrated and low calorie concentrated soft drink

Table 7.8 Energy & nutrient intakes from all food & drink by age at which household reference person ceased full-time education 2002-03

Age at which household reference person ceased full time education		Aged 14 & under	Aged 15	Aged 16	Aged 17 & under 19	Aged 19 & under 22	Aged 22 & over
Number of households in sample		971	1357	2148	1140	659	622
Average age of HRP		73	57	45	46	45	43
Average number of adults per household		1.6	1.89	1.89	1.88	1.9	1.95
Average number of children per household		0.07	0.29	0.81	0.64	0.63	0.54
Average gross weekly household income (£)		243.87	400.58	511.09	606.22	750.77	1070.97
Total energy & nutrient intakes[a]						*intakes per person per day*	
Energy	kcal	2490	2500	2200	2270	2270	2200
	MJ	10.5	10.5	9.3	9.6	9.5	9.3
Total Protein	g	81.9	85.0	74.3	76.5	76.1	75.5
Fat	g	102	103	89	92	90	87
Fatty acids:							
Saturates	g	40.7	40.2	34.8	35.8	34.9	33.5
Mono-unsaturates	g	36.8	37.5	32.1	33.1	32.6	31.2
Poly-unsaturates	g	17.6	18.2	15.5	16.6	16.1	15.9
Cholesterol	mg	292	293	244	252	250	244
Carbohydrate[b]	g	316	307	277	282	285	274
Total sugars	g	156	146	131	132	132	126
Non-milk extr sugars	g	106	101	91	90	87	79
Starch	g	159	161	146	150	153	148
Fibre[c]	g	15.4	15.2	13.3	14.3	15.0	15.4
Alcohol	g	8	12	10	12	12	13
Calcium	mg	1070	1080	960	970	960	980
Iron	mg	12.5	12.7	11.2	11.9	12.1	12.1
Zinc	mg	9.8	10.1	8.8	9.1	9.0	9.0
Magnesium	mg	293	301	265	282	286	293
Sodium[d]	g	3.06	3.37	2.97	3.02	2.86	2.82
Potassium	g	3.33	3.4	2.97	3.09	3.13	3.18
Thiamin	mg	1.70	1.74	1.55	1.63	1.64	1.64
Riboflavin	mg	2.18	2.13	1.87	1.93	1.91	1.94
Niacin Equivalent	mg	34.4	37.0	32.6	33.9	33.4	33.1
Vitamin B6	mg	2.5	2.7	2.3	2.4	2.4	2.3
Vitamin B12	µg	6.9	7.0	5.9	6.1	5.9	6.1
Folate	µg	312	312	265	287	291	302
Vitamin C	mg	72	72	65	77	86	89
Vitamin A:							
Retinol	µg	650	650	470	500	490	540
β-carotene	µg	2090	2050	1700	1870	2010	2050
Retinol equivalent	µg	1010	1000	760	820	830	890
Vitamin D	µg	4.07	3.96	3.22	3.42	3.38	3.44
Vitamin E	mg	13.03	13.47	11.62	12.35	12.24	11.94
						as a percentage of total food and drink energy	
Fat	%	37.5	37.7	36.7	36.8	36.0	35.8
Fatty acids:							
Saturates	%	15.0	14.7	14.4	14.3	14.0	13.8
Mono-unsaturates	%	13.5	13.8	13.3	13.3	13.1	12.9
Poly-unsaturates	%	6.5	6.6	6.4	6.6	6.5	6.5
Carbohydrate	%	46.9	45.3	46.6	46.0	46.8	46.3

(a) Contributions from pharmaceutical sources are not recorded by the Survey
(b) Available carbohydrate, calculated as monosaccharide
(c) As non-starch polysaccharides
(d) Excludes sodium from table salt

Ethnic origin of household reference person

There was some expectation from last year's survey that this analysis might show that one group of households had a "healthier" diet than the rest but this has not been borne out in the 2002-03 results. Nevertheless, the comparisons based on the ethnic origin of the household reference person do show that patterns in certain household food and drink purchases and in eating out can be linked to the ethnic origin of the HRP. However, when interpreting the results it should be noted that 96 per cent of the sample were "White" HRP households. Table 7.9 shows average consumption and expenditure for both household and food and drink eaten out by ethnic origin of HRP. Table 7.10 shows the average daily energy and nutrient intake from all food and drink by ethnic origin of HRP.

Household

For household food and drink, "White" HRP households continue to have the highest consumption of cheese, potatoes and alcoholic drinks, "Asian/Asian British" HRP households still consume the most cereals and fats and oils and consumption of fish and sugar and preserves remains highest in "Black/Black British" HRP households. However, members of "Chinese and other" HRP households now consume most soft drinks and "Mixed" HRP households have the highest consumption of fruit and confectionery. Household food and drink expenditure in most categories is highest in "White" HRP households where £22.59 is the average spend which is 3 per cent more than the UK average for all households. In comparison, "Chinese and other" HRP households spend £13.24 per week which is 40 per cent less than the UK average.

Eating out

Consumption of food and drink eaten out shows marked ethnic differences with members of "Black/Black British" HRP households having the lowest consumption and expenditure of most food items but "Asian/Asian British" HRP households spending the least when alcohol purchases are included. "Chinese and other" HRP household members have the highest consumption of meals eaten out whereas "White" HRP households consume the most snacks and drinks. Both groups spend similar amounts on food eaten out but "White" HRP households have the highest expenditure when alcohol purchases are taken into account.

Intakes

Households classified as "White" and "Asian/Asian British" have higher energy intakes compared to "Black/Black British", "Mixed" and "Chinese and other" households. Intakes of energy and most nutrients are highest in "White" households and are lowest in "Chinese and other" households. "White" and "Mixed" households derive the highest proportion of energy from fat and the lowest from carbohydrate whilst the reverse is true for "Asian/Asian British" and "Chinese and other" households.

Table 7.9 Consumption & expenditure of selected foods by ethnic origin of household reference person

Ethnic origin of household reference person		Asian/ Asian British	Black/ Black British	Chinese & other	Mixed	White
Number of households in sample		119	92	31	30	6328
Average age of HRP		42	45	42	40	52
Average number of adults per household		2.39	1.64	2.13	1.53	1.82
Average number of children per household		1.09	0.83	1	0.77	0.51
Average gross weekly household income (£)		603.83	370.58	530	341.8	537.08
Household consumption		*grams per person per week unless otherwise stated*				
Milk and cream	(ml)	1898	1395	1148	1617	2028
Cheese		45	51	61	108	117
Carcase meat		169	211	172	146	233
Other meat and meat products		409	715	601	698	833
Fish		135	304	119	130	154
Eggs	(no.)	1.7	1.7	1.5	1.7	1.7
Fats and oils		270	234	167	193	187
Sugar and preserves		144	172	74	159	146
Potatoes		432	656	314	419	895
Vegetables		1304	1123	993	1178	1098
Fruit		1324	1232	1210	1415	1221
Total Cereals		1962	1733	1807	1583	1663
Beverages		32	29	17	55	60
Soft drinks (a)	(ml)	1292	1889	1929	1420	1766
Alcoholic drinks	(ml)	315	349	75	490	764
Confectionery		59	66	92	149	132
Eating out consumption		*grams per person per week unless otherwise stated*				
Ethnic meals		24	18	103	30	22
Meat and meat products		55	73	100	59	96
Fish and fish products		15	10	13	11	14
Cheese and egg dishes and pizza		28	10	30	15	26
Potatoes		55	65	93	44	87
Vegetables		22	14	29	33	36
Sandwiches		73	42	56	43	82
Ice creams, desserts and cakes		23	25	27	16	33
Beverages	(ml)	111	70	82	98	150
Soft drinks including milk	(ml)	345	337	296	251	372
Alcoholic drinks	(ml)	135	290	131	284	723
Confectionery		24	20	11	17	22
Household expenditure		*pence per person per week unless otherwise stated*				
Milk and cream		120.8	94.5	89.6	110.7	151.3
Cheese		21.3	25.7	31.1	53.6	61.2
Carcase meat		74.0	80.9	58.8	51.4	108.7
Other meat and meat products		155.5	236.1	198.6	240.3	379.0
Fish		73.2	115.3	64.0	59.5	95.0
Eggs		15.1	15.3	15.9	16.3	17.4
Fats and oils		35.2	31.4	17.1	32.1	37.5
Sugar and preserves		13.4	15.5	9.0	16.2	16.3
Potatoes		63.9	65.7	46.2	59.1	101.3
Vegetables		169.2	146.8	135.5	169.5	174.2
Fruit		168.6	135.9	143.2	189.3	163.2
Total Cereals		320.8	287.4	312.2	318.4	371.8
Beverages		20.7	18.9	12.1	41.2	44.3
Soft drinks		68.7	78.9	82.7	60.4	73.7
Alcoholic drinks		111.1	83.1	6.5	135.2	265.6
Confectionery		34.4	40.7	34.6	109.0	79.5
Total all food & drink excluding alcohol		1451.3	1475.3	1317.2	1646.6	1993.6
Total all food & drink		1562.4	1558.4	1323.7	1781.9	2259.2
Eating out expenditure		*pence per person per week unless otherwise stated*				
Total all food & drink excluding alcohol		502.8	435.3	731.1	547.1	738.4
Total all food & drink		599.4	614.7	808.9	704.3	1122.6

(a) Converted to unconcentrated equivalent by applying a factor of 5 to concentrated and low calorie concentrated soft drinks

Table 7.10 Energy & nutrient intakes from all food & drink by ethnic origin of household reference person 2002-03

Ethnic origin of household reference person		Asian/ Asian British	Black/ Black British	Chinese & Other	Mixed	White
Number of households in sample		119	92	31	30	6328
Average age of HRP		42	45	42	40	52
Average number of adults per household		2.39	1.64	2.13	1.53	1.82
Average number of children per household		1.09	0.83	1	0.77	0.51
Average gross weekly household income (£)		603.83	370.58	530	341.8	537.08
Total energy & nutrient intakes[a]					*intakes per person per day*	
Energy	kcal	2260	2130	2060	2080	2320
	MJ	9.5	9.0	8.7	8.8	9.8
Total Protein	g	65.8	70.4	68.3	66.4	78.7
Fat	g	85	82	77	87	94
Fatty acids:						
Saturates	g	28.1	26.6	25.2	32.3	37.2
Mono-unsaturates	g	31	30.2	28.4	31.6	34
Poly-unsaturates	g	19.7	19.3	17.9	17	16.3
Cholesterol	mg	196	230	200	236	264
Carbohydrate[b]	g	322	288	290	265	288
Total sugars	g	113	121	103	127	138
Non-milk extr sugars	g	73	86	71	88	94
Starch	g	208	167	187	138	150
Fibre[c]	g	14.4	14.2	13.9	12.4	14.5
Alcohol	g	3	4	1	6	12
Calcium	mg	840	750	690	840	1010
Iron	mg	10.5	10.9	10.3	9.9	12.1
Zinc	mg	8	8.7	8.6	7.7	9.3
Magnesium	mg	242	259	239	240	286
Sodium[d]	g	1.71	2.10	2.10	2.37	3.13
Potassium	g	2.62	2.68	2.42	2.65	3.19
Thiamin	mg	1.43	1.44	1.29	1.31	1.65
Riboflavin	mg	1.55	1.58	1.31	1.63	2.01
Niacin Equivalent	mg	26.2	30.5	27.6	28.1	34.5
Vitamin B6	mg	2.0	2.2	1.9	1.9	2.5
Vitamin B12	µg	4.6	6.6	4.4	5.0	6.3
Folate	µg	244	268	224	246	293
Vitamin C	mg	69	77	66	78	75
Vitamin A:						
Retinol	µg	330	400	340	460	550
β-carotene	µg	1470	1460	1720	1610	1930
Retinol equivalent	µg	580	650	620	730	880
Vitamin D	µg	2.34	3.51	1.98	2.92	3.59
Vitamin E	mg	14.33	14	12.2	12.88	12.25
				as a percentage of total food and drink energy		
Fat	%	34.0	35.0	33.7	37.8	37.0
Fatty acids:						
Saturates	%	11.3	11.4	11.0	14.0	14.6
Mono-unsaturates	%	12.5	12.9	12.4	13.8	13.4
Poly-unsaturates	%	7.9	8.2	7.8	7.4	6.4
Carbohydrate	%	53.2	50.4	52.6	47.4	45.9

(a) Contributions from pharmaceutical sources are not recorded by the Survey
(b) Available carbohydrate, calculated as monosaccharide
(c) As non-starch polysaccharides
(d) Excludes sodium from table salt

Occupation of household reference person

Unlike most of the analyses in this chapter, the occupation of the HRP bears little relation to the age of the HRP and the household composition. However, the occupation of the HRP is strongly related to the average gross weekly household income and this should not be overlooked when interpreting the results. Table 7.11 shows average consumption and expenditure for both household and food and drink eaten out by occupation of the HRP. Table 7.12 shows the average daily energy and nutrient intake from all food and drink by occupation of the HRP.

Household

Weekly expenditure on household food and drink continues to be highest at £25.49 per person in households where the HRP is in the category "Higher professional". This is 16 per cent more than the UK average for all households. The lowest per capita expenditure at £15.54 is again in the category "Never worked & long-term unemployed" and this is 29 per cent lower than the UK average. The "Higher professional" households consume most cheese, fish, vegetables (excluding potatoes), fruit and alcoholic drinks whereas the "Never worked & long-term unemployed" households have the lowest consumption of all food items apart from eggs and fats and oils.

Eating out

Consumption of most food items eaten out is highest in households where the HRP is in the "Large employer, higher managerial" category. Weekly expenditure on food eaten out is also highest at £11.90 per person and represents 35 per cent of the total weekly per capita spending on all food excluding alcoholic drinks. However, when alcoholic drinks are taken into account, the highest spenders are in the "Higher professional" category where the weekly per capita expenditure on all food and drink eaten out (£17.07) represents 40 per cent of the total food and drink expenditure. The lowest weekly expenditure per person on food and drink eaten out (£9.02) is in households where the HRP is in the "Never worked and long-term unemployed" category and represents 32 per cent of their total food and drink expenditure.

Intakes

Average intakes of energy and most nutrients are lowest in "Never worked and long-term unemployed" category households. Energy intakes are highest in households where the HRP is in the "Lower supervisory & technical" category whereas the highest intakes of many vitamins and minerals are found mostly in households where the HRP is classified "Higher professional".

Table 7.11 Consumption & expenditure of selected foods by occupation of household reference person 2002-03

Occupation of household reference person		Large employer, higher managerial & professional	Small employer & own account worker	Higher professional	Intermediate	Lower professional & managerial & higher technical & supervisory	Lower supervisory & technical occupations	Never worked & long term unemployed	Routine	Semi-routine
Number of households in sample		287	396	420	419	1174	464	91	472	512
Average age of HRP		44	47	42	42	42	43	36	45	43
Average number of adults per household		2.14	2.07	2.03	1.82	2.02	2.14	1.95	2.00	1.93
Average number of children per household		0.81	0.79	0.63	0.65	0.68	0.69	0.51	0.75	0.75
Average gross weekly household income (£)		1401.32	572.71	1047.20	577.02	785.73	600.10	259.62	478.19	464.15
Household consumption								*grams per person per week unless otherwise stated*		
Milk and cream	(ml)	1758	2010	1850	1721	1828	1834	1326	1873	1992
Cheese		117	117	135	104	123	111	90	99	95
Carcase meat		199	226	196	177	215	240	143	232	210
Other meat and meat products		789	797	692	799	801	900	639	857	795
Fish		147	138	179	143	145	142	116	132	126
Eggs	(no.)	1.4	1.4	1.4	1.3	1.5	1.7	1.8	1.6	1.5
Fats and oils		150	187	150	136	157	178	195	192	179
Sugar and preserves		91	120	99	114	103	114	88	148	141
Potatoes		735	860	672	744	753	957	573	995	945
Vegetables		1107	1072	1221	954	1108	1015	806	1000	942
Fruit		1434	1101	1501	1104	1289	909	940	821	910
Total Cereals		1559	1657	1578	1531	1579	1702	1472	1678	1680
Beverages		45	51	49	44	50	49	32	52	53
Soft drinks[a]	(ml)	1846	1701	1578	1694	1895	1999	1552	1971	1987
Alcoholic drinks	(ml)	832	702	921	763	853	807	641	700	693
Confectionery		127	123	95	114	128	141	69	124	138
Eating out consumption								*grams per person per week unless otherwise stated*		
Ethnic meals		57	26	33	23	30	25	28	18	19
Meat and meat products		122	99	115	115	114	114	102	96	102
Fish and fish products		22	11	17	14	16	13	9	12	11
Cheese and egg dishes and pizza		36	24	40	29	30	29	31	32	28
Potatoes		107	90	106	91	98	94	68	90	90
Vegetables		46	33	44	40	40	33	24	30	31
Sandwiches		134	71	140	104	110	91	97	80	74
Ice creams, desserts and cakes		52	30	42	36	38	28	25	29	28
Beverages	(ml)	184	117	162	158	147	206	93	161	169
Soft drinks including milk	(ml)	517	399	520	427	466	455	522	430	423
Alcoholic drinks	(ml)	739	622	895	820	784	943	1015	841	671
Confectionery		22	26	22	29	25	27	26	32	34

(a) Converted to unconcentrated equivalent by applying a factor of 5 to concentrated and low calorie concentrated soft drink

Table 7.11 Consumption & expenditure of selected foods by occupation of household reference person 2002-03 *continued*

Occupation of household reference person	Large employer, higher managerial & professional	Small employer & own account worker	Higher professional	Intermediate	Lower professional & managerial & higher technical & supervisory	Lower supervisory & technical occupations	Never worked & long term unemployed	Routine	Semi-routine
Number of households in sample	287	396	420	419	1174	464	91	472	512
Average age of HRP	44	47	42	42	42	43	36	45	43
Average number of adults per household	2.14	2.07	2.03	1.82	2.02	2.14	1.95	2.00	1.93
Average number of children per household	0.81	0.79	0.63	0.65	0.68	0.69	0.51	0.75	0.75
Average gross weekly household income (£)	1401.32	572.71	1047.20	577.02	785.73	600.10	259.62	478.19	464.15
Household expenditure								*pence per person per week unless otherwise stated*	
Milk and cream	150.2	145.5	154.2	128.7	147.6	132.1	93.7	127.3	135.3
Cheese	66.4	61.5	81.5	52.3	67.5	51.6	43.2	44.1	45.4
Carcase meat	103.4	106.7	99.6	76.6	105.4	102.9	54.9	100.7	86.6
Other meat and meat products	418.5	368.1	388.4	366.0	397.2	383.8	249.6	347.2	334.1
Fish	103.7	84.4	113.7	78.1	94.4	79.1	58.0	67.5	67.2
Eggs	16.6	14.8	17.9	11.9	16.9	16.2	17.2	13.8	13.2
Fats and oils	34.1	35.3	34.6	26.9	33.6	29.9	27.1	31.9	31.6
Sugar and preserves	12.6	14.9	15.7	12.3	14.0	11.1	11.0	12.6	12.9
Potatoes	93.7	100.0	89.1	94.0	99.4	114.5	70.1	109.1	108.5
Vegetables	219.1	167.0	238.5	152.1	200.3	142.2	118.6	130.5	128.1
Fruit	206.1	149.1	215.1	137.8	176.4	115.0	108.1	97.5	108.1
Total Cereals	413.3	369.6	410.2	359.4	392.9	371.3	306.3	328.7	343.8
Beverages	35.5	38.9	39.5	33.4	39.1	34.2	23.3	38.0	35.1
Soft drinks	83.1	72.8	72.8	73.8	82.8	83.2	69.3	78.3	80.4
Alcoholic drinks	341.6	218.0	365.0	243.4	318.5	232.8	180.7	193.3	170.4
Confectionery	87.0	78.3	66.7	70.6	80.7	79.1	41.5	71.8	78.5
Total all food & drink excluding alcohol	2187.2	1925.7	2183.9	1781.1	2083.0	1850.9	1373.2	1700.9	1704.1
Total all food & drink	2528.9	2143.7	2548.9	2024.6	2401.5	2083.7	1553.8	1894.2	1874.5
Eating out expenditure								*pence per person per week unless otherwise stated*	
Total all food & drink excluding alcohol	1190.1	706.2	1168.9	767.3	953.5	673.5	719.5	589.3	576.0
Total all food & drink	1678.2	1038.3	1706.5	1193.4	1429.1	1127.4	1430.4	945.9	901.5

(a) Converted to unconcentrated equivalent by applying a factor of 5 to concentrated and low calorie concentrated soft drink

Table 7.12 Energy & nutrient intakes from all food & drink by occupation of household reference person 2002-03

Occupation of household reference person		Large employer, higher managerial & professional	Small employer & own account worker	Higher professional	Intermediate	Lower professional & managerial & higher technical & supervisory	Lower supervisory & technical occupations	Never worked & long term unemployed	Routine	Semi-routine
Number of households in sample		287	396	420	419	1174	464	91	472	512
Average age of HRP		44	47	42	42	42	43	36	45	43
Average number of adults per household		2.14	2.07	2.03	1.82	2.02	2.14	1.95	2.00	1.93
Average number of children per household		0.81	0.79	0.63	0.65	0.68	0.69	0.51	0.75	0.75
Average gross weekly household income (£)		1401.32	572.71	1047.20	577.02	785.73	600.10	259.62	478.19	464.15
Total energy & nutrient intakes[a]									*intakes per person per day*	
Energy	kcal	2240	2260	2230	2120	2240	2350	1920	2310	2290
	MJ	9.4	9.5	9.4	8.9	9.4	9.9	8.1	9.7	9.6
Total Protein	g	76.8	76.8	76.7	72.2	77.0	79.5	62.4	76.7	74.6
Fat	g	90	93	88	83	90	95	78	94	92
Fatty acids:										
Saturates	g	34.9	36.4	34.5	32.4	35.1	36.8	27.3	35.8	35.9
Mono-unsaturates	g	32.5	33.6	31.6	30.2	32.5	34.9	28.7	34.1	33.6
Poly-unsaturates	g	16.1	16.4	15.5	14.7	15.0	17.2	16.1	17.3	16.3
Cholesterol	mg	247	251	246	230	251	266	212	252	245
Carbohydrate[b]	g	275	279	277	268	276	289	238	291	293
Total sugars	g	129	128	129	126	131	133	103	133	136
Non-milk extr sugars	g	86	86	84	87	88	93	73	94	96
Starch	g	146	151	148	142	145	156	135	159	157
Fibre[c]	g	14.7	14.0	15.0	13.1	14.3	14.1	10.9	13.9	13.5
Alcohol	g	13	10	14	12	12	12	12	10	9
Calcium	mg	950	1000	970	910	970	990	790	970	980
Iron	mg	12.2	11.6	12.3	11.2	11.9	11.9	9.4	11.5	11.3
Zinc	mg	9	9.0	9.2	8.5	9.1	9.4	7.2	9.1	8.9
Magnesium	mg	287	273	293	260	284	281	223	272	267
Sodium[d]	g	3.02	3.00	2.97	2.88	3.08	3.19	2.44	3.10	2.98
Potassium	g	3.13	3.04	3.18	2.87	3.11	3.12	2.42	3.04	3.01
Thiamin	mg	1.64	1.61	1.65	1.54	1.64	1.63	1.31	1.60	1.56
Riboflavin	mg	1.91	1.92	1.94	1.81	1.91	1.92	1.48	1.87	1.9
Niacin Equivalent	mg	34.4	33.5	34.3	32.4	34.2	35.1	27.8	33.6	32.6
Vitamin B6	mg	2.4	2.4	2.4	2.3	2.4	2.5	1.9	2.4	2.4
Vitamin B12	µg	5.8	5.9	6.0	5.6	5.9	6.1	5.5	5.9	5.9
Folate	µg	291	281	302	267	285	281	223	274	272
Vitamin C	mg	84	70	88	69	77	65	60	61	64
Vitamin A:										
Retinol	µg	480	490	520	490	480	510	440	470	480
β-carotene	µg	1990	1860	2040	1800	1940	1780	1270	1740	1650
Retinol equivalent	µg	820	800	870	800	810	820	660	770	760
Vitamin D	µg	3.24	3.24	3.52	3.32	3.37	3.57	2.80	3.48	3.19
Vitamin E	mg	11.91	12.01	11.83	11.08	12.02	12.79	11.8	12.91	12.41
									as a percentage of total food & drink energy	
Fat	%	36.5	37.5	35.7	35.6	36.4	37.1	36.6	36.9	36.7
Fatty acids:										
Saturates	%	14.2	14.7	14.0	13.9	14.2	14.3	12.9	14.1	14.3
Mono-unsaturates	%	13.2	13.6	12.9	12.9	13.2	13.6	13.6	13.5	13.4
Poly-unsaturates	%	6.5	6.6	6.3	6.3	6.4	6.7	7.6	6.8	6.5
Carbohydrate	%	45.6	45.8	46.1	46.9	45.7	45.6	45.9	46.6	47.4

(a) Contributions from pharmaceutical sources are not recorded by the Survey
(b) Available carbohydrate, calculated as monosaccharide
(c) As non-starch polysaccharides
(d) Excludes sodium from table salt

72

Economic activity of household reference person

The economic status of the HRP is generally related to the age of the HRP, the household income and the household composition. The data shown in this analysis should be interpreted with some caution given that in "Retired" households there are practically no children. In addition, the sample size for "Government Training Scheme" households is again small which has a bearing on the precision of the estimates. Table 7.13 shows average consumption and expenditure for both household and food and drink eaten out by economic activity of the HRP. Table 7.14 shows the average daily energy and nutrient intake from all food and drink by economic activity of the HRP.

Household

Household consumption of all food items, except cheese, is again highest in "Retired" households with the lowest consumption levels being in households where the HRP is attending a Government Training Scheme. "Full-time employee" households have the highest consumption of soft and alcoholic drinks brought home and "Self-employed" households continue to eat most cheese.

The highest expenditure on food and drink brought home at £24.71 per person is in "Retired" households, which represents 78 per cent of the total weekly expenditure on all food and drink and is 13 per cent higher than the UK average for all households. "Government Training Scheme" households have the lowest per capita weekly expenditure on household food and drink at £13.82 which is 57 per cent of the total weekly expenditure and 37 per cent lower than the UK average.

Eating out

"Full-time employee" households are the highest consumers of most food items eaten out. The weekly per person eating out expenditure in these households is £13.56 which represents 38 per cent of their total weekly expenditure on all food and drink and is 24 per cent higher than the UK average for all households. Although "Government Training Scheme" households have the lowest consumption and expenditure of food eaten out, they consume and spend the most on alcoholic drinks which brings the combined spend on food and drink eaten out to 43 per cent of their overall food and drink spending. This contrasts with food and drink eaten outside the home in "ILO unemployed" households where the weekly per capita spend is £5.36, representing 26 per cent of the total amount spent on food and drink in those households.

Intakes

Households where the HRP is retired continue to have the highest energy intake and the highest intakes of almost all nutrients which reflects the absence of children in most of these households. The lowest intakes of energy and most nutrients are found in "ILO unemployed" and "Government Training Scheme" households.

Table 7.13 Consumption & expenditure of selected foods by economic activity of household reference person 2002-03

		Economically active					Economically inactive	
Economic status of household reference person		Full time employees	Part time employees	Self employed	ILO unem-ployed	Gov't Training Scheme	Retired	Other
Number of households in sample		2985	552	542	139	11	1804	892
Average age of HRP		42	45	47	41	40	74	45
Average number of adults per household		2.06	1.80	2.06	1.72	1.36	1.57	1.72
Average number of children per household		0.68	0.79	0.71	0.85	0.73	0.01	0.79
Average gross weekly household income (£)		785.96	455.49	674.43	243.46	142.64	283.04	257.15
Household consumption		*grams per person per week unless otherwise stated*						
Milk and cream	(ml)	1841	1792	2004	1559	1425	2542	2047
Cheese		116	97	122	72	90	116	97
Carcase meat		213	190	226	232	196	314	215
Other meat and meat products		814	775	774	739	740	862	781
Fish		143	137	155	114	138	221	127
Eggs	(no.)	1.5	1.6	1.4	1.8	3.0	2.2	1.9
Fats and oils		161	168	179	241	100	278	199
Sugar and preserves		109	130	122	126	117	251	180
Potatoes		821	850	806	800	480	1018	916
Vegetables		1040	1056	1134	1044	931	1359	1001
Fruit		1150	1019	1281	862	555	1659	969
Total Cereals		1617	1592	1621	1635	1597	1901	1630
Beverages		49	49	51	42	38	97	57
Soft drinks [a]	(ml)	1907	1900	1574	1423	1423	1278	1891
Alcoholic drinks	(ml)	825	642	818	491	276	583	568
Confectionery		128	116	116	99	96	149	116
Eating out consumption		*grams per person per week unless otherwise stated*						
Ethnic meals		29	26	27	20	18	9	9
Meat and meat products		117	94	100	67	58	52	69
Fish and fish products		15	13	14	8	2	16	9
Cheese and egg dishes and pizza		34	23	25	19	20	11	17
Potatoes		100	86	89	56	40	62	63
Vegetables		39	32	35	19	4	34	20
Sandwiches		110	83	78	47	57	29	37
Ice creams, desserts and cakes		36	33	33	32	16	26	22
Beverages	(ml)	176	123	125	61	128	140	87
Soft drinks including milk	(ml)	478	433	399	317	386	113	284
Alcoholic drinks	(ml)	860	671	657	318	1780	506	454
Confectionery		27	29	24	35	28	4	23
Household expenditure		*pence per person per week unless otherwise stated*						
Milk and cream		141.4	132.1	149.7	103.7	77.7	190.2	130.6
Cheese		60.7	49.3	67.9	35.9	38.0	62.5	44.2
Carcase meat		99.4	81.9	111.3	83.4	65.8	152.8	89.4
Other meat and meat products		388.8	329.8	372.7	253.6	222.9	366.9	302.6
Fish		87.8	71.2	99.3	52.0	53.5	137.7	70.6
Eggs		15.5	14.7	15.6	17.5	20.7	24.0	17.9
Fats and oils		31.6	30.8	37.7	33.7	13.9	58.8	31.8
Sugar and preserves		12.7	13.6	16.3	13.2	10.6	28.3	15.5
Potatoes		102.5	99.8	94.2	89.8	99.1	90.2	98.8
Vegetables		175.8	158.8	191.0	121.7	88.8	187.0	129.4
Fruit		152.8	130.6	178.0	99.3	61.3	223.2	118.3
Total Cereals		382.1	342.6	380.6	290.2	322.3	373.7	315.8
Beverages		37.0	35.7	39.2	28.0	22.7	66.6	39.2
Soft drinks		81.9	77.5	69.4	62.1	71.6	53.6	72.9
Alcoholic drinks		279.5	196.7	282.1	137.5	71.6	250.2	160.9
Confectionery		78.4	69.5	78.0	52.9	44.3	87.4	64.0
Total all food & drink excluding alcohol		1970.4	1747.2	2029.8	1412.8	1310.1	2221.0	1634.9
Total all food & drink		2249.9	1943.9	2311.9	1550.3	1381.7	2471.2	1795.9
Eating out expenditure		*pence per person per week unless otherwise stated*						
Total all food & drink excluding alcohol		883.8	683.1	809.5	387.9	311.6	476.0	438.7
Total all food & drink		1356.4	1054.0	1174.6	536.1	1059.9	695.8	663.9

(a) Converted to unconcentrated equivalent by applying a factor of 5 to concentrated and low calorie concentrated soft drink

Table 7.14 Energy & nutrient intakes from all food & drink by economic activity of household reference person 2002-03

		\multicolumn{5}{c	}{Economically active}	\multicolumn{2}{c}{Economically inactive}
ECONOMIC STATUS OF HOUSEHOLD REFERENCE PERSON		Full time employees	Part time employees	Self employed	ILO unemployed	Gov't Training Scheme	Retired	Other
Number of households in sample		2985	552	542	139	11	1804	892
Average age of HRP		42	45	47	41	40	74	45
Average number of adults per household		2.06	1.80	2.06	1.72	1.36	1.57	1.72
Average number of children per household		0.68	0.79	0.71	0.85	0.73	0.01	0.79
Average gross weekly household income (£)		785.96	455.49	674.43	243.46	142.64	283.04	257.15
Total energy & nutrient intakes[a]		\multicolumn{7}{r}{*intakes per person per day*}
Energy	kcal	2270	2180	2250	2120	2010	2600	2200
	MJ	9.5	9.2	9.4	8.9	8.5	10.9	9.2
Total Protein	g	77.0	72.5	77.1	67.9	70.1	87.4	72.3
Fat	g	91	87	92	91	76	107	89
Fatty acids:								
Saturates	g	35.4	33.5	36.0	32.5	28.4	43.2	34.2
Mono-unsaturates	g	33.0	31.5	33.2	33.8	27.6	38.1	32.4
Poly-unsaturates	g	16.2	15.8	16.1	18.2	15.0	17.8	16.5
Cholesterol	mg	251	237	252	230	241	313	246
Carbohydrate[b]	g	282	279	276	263	257	324	281
Total sugars	g	131	130	129	111	103	162	132
Non-milk extr sugars	g	90	91	85	76	75	106	93
Starch	g	150	148	148	152	154	162	148
Fibre[c]	g	14.1	13.5	14.4	12.4	13.2	16.7	13.0
Alcohol	g	13	10	11	6	12	10	7
Calcium	mg	970	930	990	820	810	1140	950
Iron	mg	11.9	11.2	11.8	10.1	10.9	13.4	10.8
Zinc	mg	9.1	8.6	9.1	8.2	8.5	10.5	8.7
Magnesium	mg	281	262	280	235	246	320	257
Sodium (d)	g	3.09	2.88	2.97	2.55	2.51	3.23	2.79
Potassium	g	3.09	2.95	3.1	2.66	2.49	3.63	2.91
Thiamin	mg	1.63	1.55	1.62	1.37	1.29	1.81	1.49
Riboflavin	mg	1.92	1.80	1.94	1.57	1.57	2.35	1.86
Niacin Equivalent	mg	34.3	31.9	33.7	28.7	31.5	36.8	31
Vitamin B6	mg	2.4	2.3	2.4	2.1	2.0	2.7	2.3
Vitamin B12	µg	6.0	5.7	6.0	4.9	5.1	7.7	6.1
Folate	µg	284	268	286	234	235	339	260
Vitamin C	mg	73	68	76	55	44	86	64
Vitamin A:								
Retinol	µg	500	460	490	380	290	770	480
β-carotene	µg	1850	1740	1960	1580	1330	2290	1640
Retinol equivalent	µg	810	760	820	650	510	1160	760
Vitamin D	µg	3.42	3.18	3.30	2.93	2.55	4.34	3.21
Vitamin E	mg	12.18	11.92	11.84	13.2	10.46	13.19	12.21
		\multicolumn{7}{r}{*as a percentage of total food & drink energy*}
Fat	%	36.5	36.2	37.2	38.9	34.2	37.6	37.1
Fatty acids:								
Saturates	%	14.2	14.0	14.6	14.0	12.7	15.2	14.2
Mono-unsaturates	%	13.3	13.1	13.5	14.5	12.4	13.5	13.5
Poly-unsaturates	%	6.5	6.6	6.5	7.8	6.8	6.3	6.8
Carbohydrate	%	46.0	47.4	45.5	46.2	47.6	46.1	47.3

(a) Contributions from pharmaceutical sources are not recorded by the Survey
(b) Available carbohydrate, calculated as monosaccharide
(c) As non-starch polysaccharides
(d) Excludes sodium from table salt

Chapter 8: Related official statistics

Comparison of dietary surveys

As well as the Expenditure and Food Survey the National Diet and Nutrition Survey collects data on food consumption. Also the Health Survey for England and the Health Survey for Scotland collect data on consumption of fruit and vegetables.

Estimates of consumption and intake vary across the surveys due to differences between the surveys in population covered and method of collection. Population may be United Kingdom or England and all people or adults or children. The method of collection varies from diaries of household expenditure to 24 hour recall of what was consumed. Each survey method has its merits.

The Expenditure and Food Survey (previously the National Food Survey)

The Expenditure and Food Survey collects data on expenditure and quantities of food purchased for both household purchases and food and drink eaten out. For food eaten out the quantities are based on standard portion sizes. Nutritional content is obtained by converting consumption into nutrient intakes based on nutrient profiles for each type of food, allowance being made for wastage.

- Strengths: Estimates are produced every year and for household food consumption go back to 1940. The data can be analysed by geographical area and social/demographic characteristics. The food component of the survey is cost efficient and produces timely estimates, normally about one year after the end of data collection. Misreporting which is generally a problem in dietary surveys is minimised by basing the collection at the level of the household and on expenditure rather than consumption.
- Weaknesses: It only provides estimates of average consumption per person and cannot be used to directly estimate more detailed aspects of individuals' consumption, for example how many people are consuming less or more than recommended levels.
- Response: The responding sample for the 2002/03 survey was 6,927 households across the UK. Response to the survey currently runs at 60 per cent of those selected. Historically it has been higher as for other government surveys.

The National Diet and Nutrition Survey

The National Diet and Nutrition Survey collects information about the diet and nutritional status of individuals in Britain. Food consumption data are collected on individual weighed intakes of food over a 4 to 7 day period. Nutritional content is based on conversion factors for each different type of food. The survey is run in a regular programme covering four discrete age groups about every 2-3 years.

- Strengths: Estimates are of food eaten (as opposed to purchased) by individuals. The data can be analysed by individuals' characteristics and by region and by demographic categories.
- Weaknesses: There is only limited scope for time series (the survey covering adults was run in 1986-87 and 2001). Under-reporting of habitual intake is a known problem with dietary surveys, particularly those involving weighing the food.
- Response: Response in the 2001 survey of adults was 47 per cent.
- The Food Standards Agency is developing proposals for a revised National Diet and Nutrition Survey based on a rolling programme.

The Health Survey for England

Consumption of fruit and vegetables is collected using a questionnaire to record individuals' recollected consumption in the previous 24 hours. Portion sizes are based on individuals' perceptions. Additional and wide ranging information on health, varying from year to year, is also collected.

- Strengths: Data on fruit and vegetable consumption can be analysed by individuals' health attributes. The survey questions are designed to capture portions qualifying for the 5 A DAY programme (aimed at getting everyone to eat five portions of fruit and vegetables a day).
- Weakness: It only covers fruit and vegetables (food consumption is not the primary purpose of the survey). Overestimation of perceived healthy behaviours is a common problem of recall methods.
- Response: Data on fruit and vegetable consumption are only available since 2000.

The Scottish Health Survey

It contains a section on "eating habits" which is similar to the Health Survey for England. It asks about patterns of consumption of a wide range of food types including fruit and vegetables. Seven major food types are asked about: foods containing sugar, spreading and cooking fats, dairy produce, meat and poultry, fish, foods containing starch and fibre, and fresh fruit and vegetables. Respondents are asked to say, for example, how often they eat fresh fruit and prompted with 9 categories of answer from "6 or more times a day" to "less often or never".

- Strength: the survey includes biological measures of health that can be linked to diet, such as cholesterol measures.
- Weakness: It does not provide a detailed measure of consumption or of nutritional value but instead provides more general estimates of 'eating habits' and patterns.

- Response: The first Scottish Health survey was in 1995 and then 1998. The 2003-04 survey is currently being done. In 1998 9047 adults aged 16 to 64 and 3892 children took part. The response rate was 77 per cent of eligible households.

When to use Each Survey

For clarity this is presented as a series of questions and answers.

Q. What are the best estimates of consumption of fruit and vegetables?

A. All three surveys provide useful information. You have to be more specific about what exactly you want to know. Examples of the types of information provided by each survey are given below.

Q. What are the long term trends in fruit and vegetable consumption?

A. Use the Expenditure and Food Survey results with household consumption going back to 1942.

Q. Are some types of people eating very little fruit and vegetables?

A. Use the National Diet and Nutrition Survey for individual levels of consumption compared with their personal characteristics. The Expenditure and Food Survey can be used to see how consumption of all members of a household varies by household characteristics such as income, region and ethnicity.

Q. Are those that eat more fruit and vegetables healthier?

A. None of the surveys is designed or able to answer this as they do not measure health outcomes like death, cancer or heart disease with a longitudinal component. Use the Health Survey for England to analyse individuals' consumption by their health characteristics or the National Diet and Nutrition Survey which gives details of people's nutrition status as well as food and nutrient intake.

Q. How many portions of fruit and vegetables per day are people eating on average?

A. The Health Survey for England and the Health Survey for Scotland record consumption of items in the way that they count towards the 5 A DAY programme. The Expenditure and Food Survey gives trends over time of portions per day averaged over the population but cannot exclude fruit juice and baked beans above the allowed thresholds in the 5 A DAY programme. The latest National Diet and Nutrition Survey of adults also provides information on the number of portions of fruit and vegetables consumed by this age group according to the 5 A DAY definition. Note that a portion of fruit and vegetables is defined as 80 grams.

Q. Do the Expenditure and Food Survey and the National Diet and Nutrition Survey produce similar estimates of food consumption?

A. It is not possible to compare the surveys directly in terms of types of food consumed because the EFS results are by types of food purchased and the NDNS results are by types of food eaten. For example the EFS records sugars and oils as they are purchased whereas in the NDNS these items are recorded within the finished food product, e.g. home made cake.

Q. Do the Expenditure and Food Survey and the National Diet and Nutrition Survey produce similar estimates of nutritional intake?

A. Broadly, yes. But because the surveys record different aspects of food consumption, and use different populations and methods, they are not identical.

Q. Do the Expenditure and Food Survey and the Health Survey for England produce similar estimates of average number of portions of fruit and vegetables per day?

A. Broadly, yes.

Comparison of estimates of percentage energy from fat and saturated fatty acids

According to the National Diet and Nutrition Survey of adults aged 19 to 64, men derived a mean of 35.8 per cent and women 34.9 per cent of their food energy intake from fat in 2000-01. This compares with a complete UK population average from the Expenditure and Food Survey in 2002-03 of 37.6 per cent of food energy from fat. In both cases energy from alcohol has been excluded.

Similarly, according to the National Diet and Nutrition Survey, men derived 13.4 per cent and women 13.2 per cent of their food energy intake from saturated fatty acids. The population estimate from the Expenditure and Food Survey in 2002-03 is 14.7 per cent.

The Expenditure and Food Survey estimates are appreciably higher. This may be because the Expenditure and Food Survey covers the whole UK population and includes sections outside the National Diet and Nutrition Survey, specifically people and children under 19 years old and people over 64 years old. It may also be because the Expenditure and Food Survey measures food purchases at the household level as opposed to food consumed by individuals. However under-reporting is a known problem in all dietary surveys and may be another factor.

Comparison of estimates of fruit and vegetable consumption

According to the Health Survey for England on average 3.4 portions of fruit and vegetables were consumed per person per day for adults aged 16 and over in England in 2002.

An estimate from the Expenditure and Food Survey for 2002-03 is an average of 4.1 portions per day (based on 2305 grams per week at 80 grams per portion). However, this estimate covers everyone in the UK and also includes all fruit juices and all baked beans, as opposed to a maximum of 80 grams per person of each. It also measures food weight as purchased rather than as eaten.

Family Spending

The Expenditure and Food Survey also underlies the ONS publication "Family Spending". The estimate of household expenditure on food and non-alcoholic drinks reported in "Family Spending" of £42.70 per household per week in 2002-03 is not entirely consistent with the estimates published in this report. Both are based on the same survey data but they are weighted in different ways to become representative of households (for "Family Spending") or people (for "Family Food"). A simple conversion from per person to per household is possible based on the average number of people per household in the population, but this results in a slightly less precise estimate for households than that given in "Family Spending". "Family Spending" can be obtained from the Office for National Statistics website.

Table 8.1 Reconciliation of Family Food and Family Spending

Reconciliation of average expenditure in Family Food and Family Spending for 2002-03		
Family Spending Estimate of Expenditure on food and non-alcoholic drink[a]	£42.70	per household per week
Family Food Estimate of Expenditure		
on all food and drink	£21.91	per person per week
less alcoholic drink	£2.49	per person per week
less takeaways brought home	£1.46	per person per week
equals adjusted expenditure[b]	£17.96	per person per week
survey person count estimate (million)	24.35	
survey household count (million)	57.9904	
persons per household in the survey	2.38	
adjusted expenditure on food and drink[b]	£42.78	per household per week

(a) excludes takeaway food
(b) covers the same food and drink items as the Family Spending estimate

Food prices

The ONS publish indices of food prices which form part of the Retail Price Index (RPI). Food prices rose according to the food components of the RPI by 2.1 per cent between April 2002 and March 2003, the period covered by the Expenditure and Food Survey.

From the Expenditure and Food Survey one can derive an implied price by dividing the estimate of expenditure on household food by the corresponding estimate of consumption. This is more appropriately called a unit value because it measures the value per unit of everything that was purchased. In contrast the retail price index measures the change in price of a fixed basket of goods.

According to the Expenditure and Food Survey there was a 1.9 per cent increase in the unit value of household food purchases excluding confectionery, soft drinks and alcoholic drinks in 2002-03. In contrast there was a drop in the food price index (excludes alcoholic drinks) of -0.3 per cent in 2002-03.

Large discrepancies include seasonal foods, bread, biscuits, butter and soft drinks. All of these apart from soft drinks are estimated to have increased in unit value by more than their corresponding component in the RPI. This suggests a consumer switch to more expensive products, probably of higher quality.

Table 8.2 Price changes between 2001-02 and 2002-03

Price and unit value changes between 2001-02 and 2002-03

percentage changes	unit value prices in EFS	prices from RPI
ALL ITEMS RPI		2.1
ALL ITEMS EXCEPT FOOD		2.4
FOOD	1.9	-0.3
SEASONAL FOOD	0.6	-4.6
BREAD	4.2	1.5
CEREALS	-1.6	-0.6
BISCUITS & CAKES	4.3	1.1
BEEF	1.9	-0.5
LAMB	6.4	6.5
PORK	2.8	3.1
BACON	-2.4	-2.5
POULTRY	2.7	-2.2
FISH	1.5	1.3
BUTTER	4.6	-0.2
CHEESE	2.3	0.1
EGGS	2.1	-2.6
MILK	3.9	2.3
TEA	0.5	1.8
COFFEE & HOT DRINKS	-1.1	-1.0
SOFT DRINKS	-33.1	-0.6
SUGAR & PRESERVES	4.8	2.7
SWEETS & CHOCOLATES	-4.4	3.1
POTATOES	-8.9	-5.9
VEGETABLES	1.2	-0.9
FRUIT	1.2	-0.3
of which FRESH FRUIT	0.9	-0.8

Consumer Trends

The ONS publishes estimates of household final consumption expenditure including expenditure on food and drink within its flagship publication "Consumer Trends". The food estimates are based upon the Expenditure and Food Survey but are not fully compatible with the estimates presented here. They are adjusted to be compatible with National Accounts. They also differ in that they show total expenditure over a specified period as opposed to average expenditure per person per week.

Chapter 9: Adjustments to the National Food Survey estimates

Background

In April 2001, the Expenditure and Food Survey replaced the Family Expenditure Survey and the National Food Survey. For some types of food, particularly snack foods and alcoholic drinks, the National Food Survey estimates of expenditure were considerably lower than in the Expenditure and Food Survey.

The Expenditure and Food Survey estimates are broadly comparable with historic Family Expenditure Survey estimates but not with historic National Food Survey estimates, probably due to the similarity in methodology of the Expenditure and Food Survey and the Family Expenditure Survey.

In the National Food Survey there was one main diary keeper who recorded all expenditure and consumption. In the Expenditure and Food Survey, following the Family Expenditure Survey methodology, all household members from the age of seven years record their expenditure in personal diaries. Furthermore the diary is simpler in that it records details of purchases only and not the additional burden of consumption of items not purchased.

Therefore Defra decided to adjust the historical estimates from the National Food Survey so that the adjusted estimates of expenditure would be comparable with the expenditure estimates from the Family Expenditure Survey. This process reduces the problem of under-reporting in the National Food Survey.

Estimates from the Family Expenditure Survey in 2000 are available for expenditure on each of 65 types of food. Corresponding estimates were constructed from the National Food Survey. The differences in the estimates, after accounting for demographic and socio-economic differences in the samples, were used to determine the adjustment factors.

ONS project of deriving multiplicative adjustment factors

Defra commissioned the ONS to carry out a project to devise a way of correcting the NFS diary data. The study carried out a statistical analysis comparing FES and NFS results in 2000 (1999 and 1998 were also looked at but it was decided to use the 2000 analysis only). In order to make this comparison, NFS food codes had to be mapped to FES food codes. The result was a set of 65 codes based on FES to which the more than 200 NFS codes were mapped. In addition, demographic and socio-economic variables used in deriving the factors needed to be made comparable.

The essence of the method was to compare FES and NFS diary data. Four variables were found to be associated with the under-reporting: age of the main diary keeper (7 age groups), income band (5 income bands), government office region (13 regions) and household composition (11 groups). The method produced a different factor for each of the variables and each of the mapped food codes. Thus, (5+7+13+11)*65=2340 different factors were derived from the 2000 NFS and EFS datasets. The factors were applied by multiplication with the quantity and cost variables recorded in the diary. Each diary entry was multiplied by the appropriate food code factors for age of main diary keeper, income band, government office region and household composition.

Defra original scaling (published in October 2003)

The 2340 factors derived using NFS data for 2000 were intended to be used on previous years' NFS datasets. Unfortunately using the factors on the diary data for years other than 2000 produced unstable results due to extrapolation beyond the range of the 2000 data (i.e. some combinations of the variables were not present in 2000 but were in previous years). Therefore, a second set of factors was derived based on the adjusted estimates of average consumption and average expenditure across the UK for the year 2000. These adjusted UK averages were compared to the original NFS UK averages for 2000 for 24 groupings of foods and an adjustment factor derived for each grouping. These factors were then used to adjust the datasets for earlier years. The 24 factors were published in "Family Food 2001-02".

Defra revised scaling

Problems were identified with the original adjustments mainly due to heterogeneity within the 24 food groupings. The solution was to allow a different adjustment for each individual food code in the 2000 year NFS dataset.

Applying the adjustments back to 1974

The method is based on the assumption that the percentage of under-reporting has not changed significantly between 1974 and 2000. The overall level of under-reporting turns out to be lower in 1974 because the foods most prone to under-reporting were less common then.

Because food codes have changed over the years it was necessary to construct factors for the codes that are not present in the 2000 dataset. Factors for these other codes were derived on an 'ad hoc' basis. Each entry in the original NFS diary data for the years from 1974 to 2000 was multiplied by the adjustment factor from the extended list of minor food codes. These datasets were aggregated to form UK averages for each NFS minor food code as they existed in the respective years. Nutrient and energy intakes were derived by applying the appropriate nutrient conversion factors.

Finally the estimates of consumption and expenditure in NFS format were converted into EFS codes. Each NFS code was mapped either directly to an EFS food code or distributed across more than one EFS code.

The adjustment factors for each individual National Food Survey food code and the mapping into Expenditure and Food Survey codes are available on the Defra website.

Impact of the adjustments

Table 9.1 compares the adjusted National Food Survey estimates for the year 2000 with unadjusted estimates. The adjusted estimate for confectionery is more than double (2.37 times) the size of the unadjusted estimate. This indicates considerable under-reporting in the National Food Survey probably due mainly to difficulties capturing instances of snacks where there is just one diary keeper. The adjustments for alcoholic drinks, beverages and sugar and preserves are also significant but not as large.

In general the adjustments have had the effect of increasing the estimates but for eggs and carcass meat the adjusted estimates are lower. In the case of eggs the estimates of expenditure from the Family Expenditure Survey were on average 8 per cent lower than the estimates from the National Food Survey. The reasons for differences in the two surveys include the sampling design, the questionnaire design, the keying, the coding and the validation procedures.

Energy intake in the year 2000 has been adjusted upwards by 14 per cent and most nutrient intakes adjusted upwards by about 10 per cent. Added sugars and alcohol have been adjusted upwards by 30 per cent and 62 per cent respectively in line with their dependence on confectionery and alcoholic drinks.

Table 9.2 shows the adjustments to the 1974 estimates. The impact is smaller mainly because confectionery, soft drinks and alcoholic drinks were not collected then and have large adjustments in 2000. However the impact is also reduced because there were fewer purchases in 1974 of items with high adjustments.

Table 9.1 Impact of adjustments to the National Food Survey in 2000

Comparison of adjusted and unadjusted National Food Survey estimates

		unadjusted 2000	adjusted 2000	ratio
HOUSEHOLD CONSUMPTION		\multicolumn{2}{r}{*per person per week*}	
Milk and cream	(ml)	2087	2164	1.04
Cheese	g	109	109	1.00
Carcase meat	g	248	235	0.95
Other meat and meat products	g	716	779	1.09
Fish	g	141	144	1.02
Eggs	(no.)	1.8	1.6	0.92
Fats and oils	g	188	193	1.03
Sugar and preserves	g	139	167	1.20
Potatoes	g	922	1002	1.09
Vegetables	g	1072	1147	1.07
Fruit	g	1111	1189	1.07
Total Cereals	g	1516	1698	1.12
Beverages	g	57	70	1.22
Soft drinks [a]	(ml)	1533	1699	1.11
Alcoholic drinks	(ml)	430	725	1.69
Confectionery	g	64	151	2.37
Household Intakes [e]			*per person per day*	
Energy	kcal	1881	2152	1.14
	MJ	8	9	1.14
Total Protein	g	67	72	1.07
Fat	g	76	86	1.13
Fatty acids: Saturates	g	30	35	1.14
Mono-unsaturates	g	27	31	1.14
Poly-unsaturates	g	14	15	1.11
Cholesterol	mg	225	236	1.05
Carbohydrate [b]	g	239	277	1.16
including Total sugars	g	108	131	1.22
Non-milk extr sugars	g	67	88	1.30
starch	g	131	145	1.11
Fibre [c]	g	13	14	1.10
Alcohol	g	4	7	1.62
Calcium	mg	887	967	1.09
Iron	mg	10	11	1.10
Zinc	mg	8	9	1.07
Magnesium	mg	239	266	1.12
Sodium [d]	g	2.606	2.896	1.11
Potassium	g	2.721	3.006	1.10
Thiamin	mg	1	2	1.07
Riboflavin	mg	2	2	1.08
Niacin Equivalent	mg	29	31	1.07
Vitamin B6	mg	2	2	1.06
Vitamin B12	µg	6	6	1.07
Folate	µg	252	269	1.06
Vitamin C	mg	64	70	1.09
Vitamin A: Retinol	µg	499	613	1.23
Carotene	µg	1760	1906	1.08
Retinol equivalent	µg	793	931	1.17
Vitamin D	µg	3	3	1.04
Vitamin E	mg	10	11	1.13

(a) Converted to unconcentrated equivalent by applying a factor of 5 to concentrated and low calorie concentrated soft drinks
(b) Available carbohydrate, calculated as monosaccharide
(c) As non-starch polysaccharides
(d) Excludes sodium from table salt
(e) Contributions from pharmaceutical sources are not recorded by the Survey

Table 9.2 Impact of adjustments to the National Food Survey in 1974

Comparison of adjusted and unadjusted National Food Survey estimates

		unadjusted 1974	adjusted 1974	ratio
Household consumption		\multicolumn{3}{l}{*per person per week*}	
Milk and cream	(ml)	2897	2978	1.03
Cheese	g	105	105	1.00
Carcase meat	g	413	393	0.95
Other meat and meat products	g	606	630	1.04
Fish	g	123	123	1.01
Eggs	(no.)	4.1	3.7	0.92
Fats and oils	g	316	316	1.00
Sugar and preserves	g	441	535	1.21
Potatoes	g	1374	1437	1.05
Vegetables	g	1073	1141	1.06
Fruit	g	670	731	1.09
Total Cereals	g	1629	1842	1.13
Beverages	g	91	107	1.18
Household Intakes [a]		\multicolumn{3}{l}{*per person per day*}	
Energy	kcal	2326	2534	1.09
	MJ	10	11	1.09
Total Protein	g	71	74	1.04
Fat	g	106	111	1.05
Fatty acids: Saturates	g	51	52	1.03
Mono-unsaturates	g	40	42	1.05
Poly-unsaturates	g	11	12	1.09
Carbohydrate [b]	g	287	327	1.14
Calcium	mg	1012	1067	1.06
Iron	mg	12	13	1.11
Thiamin	mg	1	1	1.06
Riboflavin	mg	2	2	1.07
Niacin Equivalent	mg	29	30	1.05
Vitamin C	mg	51	54	1.06
Vitamin A: Retinol	µg	775	1008	1.30
Carotene	µg	2154	2272	1.05
Retinol equivalent	µg	1228	1480	1.20
Vitamin D	µg	9	9	1.03

(a) Contributions from pharmaceutical sources are not recorded by the Survey
(b) Available carbohydrate, calculated as monosaccharide.